SEATTLE
A PICTORIAL HISTORY

SEATTLE

A PICTORIAL HISTORY

By Lane Morgan and Murray Morgan
with Paul Dorpat

Design by Jamie Backus Raynor

This picture of the Seattle waterfront in 1878 was created by Paul Dorpat from three photographs taken by Peterson & Brother. Denny Hill is on the skyline to the left. The large white house with a second story porch at the foot of the hill belongs to Roland Denny; Arthur Denny lived next door to the right. The Territorial University with cupola and columns is atop Denny's Knoll. Below it, to the left, is the Congregation Church and to the right the Protestant Methodist Church. The large gray structure on the waterfront at the foot of Madison Street is the Pontius Building, where the great Seattle fire started in 1889. Courtesy of Paul Dorpat and Photograph Collection, University of Washington Library

DONNING COMPANY/PUBLISHERS NORFOLK/VA BEACH

Library of Congress Cataloging in Publication
Data
Morgan, Lane, 1949-
    Seattle, a pictorial history.
    Bibliography: p.
    Includes index.
    1. Seattle—Description—Views. 2. Seattle—
History—Pictorial works. I. Morgan, Murray
Cromwell, 1916 - joint author. II. Title.
F899.S443M67   979.7'77   80-27645
ISBN 0-89865-091-7 (pbk.)

Printed in the United States of America

FOR ROSA
Patron saint of works in progress

CONTENTS

The Woodward Granary and the Occidental Brotherhood occupied the three story warehouse on the outboard side of Cliff Avenue at the foot of Marion Street. Central School is on the skyline above it. To the right of Central School can be seen the blunt steeple of the Presbyterian Church. Far to the right, at the foot of Columbia Street, is the Elephant Store. Behind it, slightly to the right, is the Methodist Episcopal Church. Courtesy of Paul Dorpat and Photograph Collection, University of Washington Library

FOREWORD

Lane Morgan and her father, Murray Morgan, were born in Tacoma, thirty-three years apart. Neither lives in Seattle now, Lane having her home in Sumas, up by the British Columbia border, and Murray holing up in a remodelled dance hall somewhere around Federal Way. But daughter and father share a fascination with Seattle, past and present.

Murray's *Skid Road,* written in 1951, remains the book newcomers are most likely to be given by old-timers to explain why we Seattle folk are the way we are. Lane, after valiant years spent bringing the Seattle *Argus* ("oldest weekly west of the Mississippi") into the twentieth century, edits *The Northwest Experience,* a twice-yearly assemblage of articles about the possibilities and threats inherent in living around here.

In this collaboration, Lane and Murray trace the growth of Seattle from its bedraggled beginnings on Alki Point to the state of being it has reached, an approximation of perfection that has led some of us to raise the banner of Lesser Seattle and set our eyes not upon growth but eternity.

Emmett Watson

ACKNOWLEDGEMENTS

A photo-history is by nature a collaboration. It involves not only writers, photographers, librarians and archivists of the period when it is prepared but those who recorded the past when it was the living present. Assembling such a book is happy work.

Nothing in this project has given us greater pleasure than our association with Paul Dorpat, whose knowledge of the photographic history of Seattle is exceeded only by the generosity with which he shares the fruits of his research. Paul's affair with Seattle's past began years ago when he looked up the history of a building a friend had acquired. That specific quest turned into a lasting passion, and Paul became an ambulatory archive. To walk with him down a Seattle street, to drive along the waterfront, to look at the blow-ups on his studio wall above a wallboard warehouse, or to visit one of his exhibits is to see the city with a fourth dimension. Past and present, what was, what might have been, what yet might be, exist together. Henry Yesler rubs shoulders with Dave Beck; Bill Speidel is photographed on the same spot where his hero, Doc Maynard, stood for a portrait by Sammis; Princess Angeline is sister to Nellie Cornish; the *Eliza Anderson* and the Boeing 747 have a kinship. The window you are looking out opens not on today's First Avenue but Front Street and the roof of the Pontius Building where the 1889 fire began. You realize for the first time that the hills you see you would not have seen before That Man Thomson levelled Denny Hill.

Paul's concern with the lay of the land, and the occasional rape of it, is felt throughout this book, as is his unstinting help in locating pictures by cameramen of other eras whose works are not in the public collections.

Dennis Andersen's loving familiarity with the Photographic Collection of the University of Washington Library transformed our vague memories of pictures we'd once seen into glossies in hand. Nancy Pryor of the Northwest Collection of the Washington State Library in Olympia and Jean Coberly of the historical section of the Seattle Public Library shared their expertise as well as the photo files in their custody. Jeanne Engerman of the Washington State Historical Society in Tacoma was of great help in identifying photographs.

The Seattle *Post-Intelligencer* and the Tacoma *News Tribune* made photographs available from

their morgues. The Boeing Company was most generous with material in its historical files. Fred Short, Rodger Collins and Ed Ribback helped locate pictures in the Port of Seattle collection, as did Jack Crider of Seattle City Light, and Eleanor Toews of the Seattle Public Schools archives. Al Brisbois made available photos gathered by the Pacific Northwest Labor History Association. Roger Soder of the Seattle Urban League supplied both pictures and information.

The late Robert Hitchman, an authority on Seattle's past, was unfailingly helpful, making pictures available and offering excellent advice. Edward and Elizabeth Burke helped with pictures and information about the International District.

John and Lael Hanawalt, whose Old Seattle Paperworks in the Pike Place Market is a joy to collectors, opened their files and added to our knowledge. Mr. and Mrs. Frederick Mann, who have the Ambrose Kiehl collection in their custody, helped us obtain permission from Laura Kiehl for the first publication of some of his works. Grace Loudon McAdam made possible the reproduction of several of her brother's pictures from the World War I period, including one in which she was a showgirl. Jean Hudson Lunzer of the Seattle Post-Intelligencer allowed the use of photographs by her father, Will Hudson.

Lou Miller, whose collection of Webster & Stevens photographs includes mint-condition specimens of pictures familiar in foggier reproductions, allowed the use of some of his classics. Johsel Namkung made a special print of the portrait of Mark Tobey, one of the artist's favorite pictures of himself. Werner Lenggenhager, long-time recorder of Seattle architecture, made available a classic shot of the Freeway fountain. The antique dealer, Gerald Johnson, permitted reproductions from the Baron Duffy album in his possession.

Others whose help is remembered with appreciation include Sara Levant of Madrona Publishers, May Sasaki, Henry Gordon of the Fremont *Forum,* Gordon Clinton, Eric Scigliano, Chuck Nacke, Harold V. Smith, Gladys Shillestad Kayshor, Ruby Sheurman Wells, Butch Nelson, Inga Stanvik and Gary Reese. Special thanks for hospitality to Carolyn Marr and Nile Thompson, Rinjing Dorje and Yeshe Dolma, and Susan Chadwick, and to Bruce Brown for holding the fort.

THE SITE OF SEATTLE 1850.

From West Shore, October 1889; courtesy of Photograph Collection, University of Washington Library

INTRODUCTION/ BEGINNINGS

To the west, Puget Sound; beyond the water, the Olympics. To the east, the long stretch of Lake Washington; beyond, the Cascades. To the north, unbroken forest, climaxed on clear days by Mount Baker. To the south, a lush valley laced with rivers and streams, rising to the ethereal bulk of Mount Rainier. The setting for what became Seattle was indeed lovely, but the first whites to pass its way paid slight attention. There were so many bays, so many vistas, so much forest.

The officers of the British ships *Discovery* and *Chatham,* which anchored off Bainbridge Island in May of 1792, wrote of "masts and spars for all the navies of the world," speculated about the rewards of agriculture in land that sustained such magnificent trees, praised the splendid anchorage in Port Orchard, but none noted anything special about the hilly land eastward across the sound. Nor did the party of Hudson's Bay Company men who rowed past the future Seattle in December of 1824 while pioneering the small-boat route between the Columbia and Fraser rivers, though they landed at Three Tree Point and complained of "weighty rain."

Not until July 9, 1833, did anyone describe the site in writing. Then William Fraser Tolmie, a young Scottish physician visiting the Hudson's Bay Company post under construction north of the Nisqually River, came by canoe to look at the open land fur traders had said might make a good trading post. He landed at Alki Point.

Tolmie wrote in his journal: "It was about a mile in length & from 100 to 150 yards in extent, raised about thirty feet above the sea level, toward which it presented a steep clayey bank, surface flat and dotted with tall pines, but soil composed almost entirely of sand. South side of bay and [Duwamish] River is inhabited by Tuamish indians, of whom we saw several parties along the coast miserably poor and destitute of firearms....A Fort well garrisoned would answer well as a trading post [but for] an unproductive soil and the inconvenience of going at least ½ mile for a supply of water. Breakfasted on pease eaten with a shell out of a pot lid." Nothing further came of Tolmie's visit.

Seattle's first settlers were brought to Alki Point from Portland on the Exact, a seventy-three-foot schooner which had been built in Nantucket and brought around Cape Horn to San Francisco in the early days of the Gold Rush. Finding the bay almost a boardwalk of ships seeking cargo east, Captain Isaiah Folger gave up on the Golden Gate and came north to the Columbia River in 1851. He had chartered the Exact to a group of overly optimistic prospectors intent on reaching the Queen Charlotte Islands when Arthur Denny displayed ready cash and Folger agreed to make a detour and deposit the pioneers mid-way down Puget Sound. Painter unknown; courtesy of Photograph Collection, University of Washington Library

Americans first appeared in May of 1841 when the sloop-of-war *Porpoise* of the Wilkes Expedition sent a longboat into the bay to check its depths and chart its banks. Lieutenant Wilkes later gave the place its name, Elliott Bay, presumably for Midshipman Samuel B. Elliott, a member of the survey crew.

Not until the Treaty of 1846 established the boundary between British and American possessions in the Pacific Northwest did any whites come to settle. The first to seek a homestead was a nineteen-year-old farmer, John Holgate. He chose farmland up the Duwamish in today's Georgetown, but neglected to file his claim before returning east on a visit. When he came back another farmer, Luther Collins, was on his chosen site, so he selected another on Beacon Hill.

On September 25, 1851, three young men who were not primarily concerned with farmland disembarked at the mouth of the Duwamish from a sailing scow whose owner was buying salmon from the Indians. Thirty-one-year-old John Low and nineteen-year-old David Denny were scouts for two groups from Illinois who had teamed up on the Oregon Trail. When they found the best lands in the Willamette Valley already claimed and Portland, with its 2,000 inhabitants, over-populated and over-priced, they sent Low and Denny to check out Puget Sound. In Olympia they met Lee Terry, a twenty-year-old New Yorker who, having failed to find gold in California, was now prospecting for a site that might develop into a city.

It was a common dream. Faith and a bit of flat land near a waterway were enough to make many a pioneer imagine a metropolis. With enough faith you could imagine the land to be flat. By the time the skipper of the scow dropped his three passengers at Duwamish Head, Terry had his companions thinking urban.

Terry and Low made a cursory inspection of the lower Duwamish from an Indian dugout. Denny examined the south shore of the bay and made acquaintance with the local Indian leader, whose name the whites came to spell "Seattle." The next day the scouting party met Luther Collins, who was bringing his wife and daughter up from the Nisqually to his new claim on the Duwamish.

Collins exulted in the farming potential of the bottomland, whose floods he had yet to experience. His confidence was catching. Terry, Low, and Denny agreed the Duwamish would become a garden spot and that a city at the mouth of the river would control its trade. With wild assurance they agreed to Terry's suggestion that the great city of the west should be called "New York."

Low hired Denny and Terry to build a cabin while he went back to Portland to tell the rest of the Illinois party of their good luck. David sent a note to his older brother, Arthur. "We have examined the valley of the Duwamish River and find it a fine country. There is room for 1,000 settlers. Come at once."

Twenty-two of the anticipated thousand arrived from the Columbia River on November 13, aboard the schooner *Exact*. There were ten adults, the oldest thirty-four years, and twelve children, the youngest two months. They were rowed ashore in a steady rain to find the cabin unroofed (there had been no frow to split shingles) and David Denny alone (Terry had set off three weeks earlier to buy some tools). David was suffering from malaria, neuralgia, an axe wound in the foot, and poor spirits. "I wish you hadn't come, but I'm glad to see you," he told them, adding, "The skunks have gotten in and eaten all my provisions." The women wept. The men set out to subdivide.

The newcomers soon decided New York was mislocated. The soil on the point was poor. Their only source of cash was lumber for the San Francisco market, but the beach was too shallow to permit easy loading. They needed deeper water. Soundings made from a canoe with a bunch of horseshoes tied to a clothesline revealed deeper water along the eastern shore. Most of the party moved across the bay, though Lee Terry, who had been joined by his brother, Charles, and Low stayed on the spit they now called New York Alki, meaning in the Chinook jargon, New York by-and-by.

Joined first by David Maynard, an Ohio physician and promoter of considerable charm and high alcoholic content, and then by Henry Yesler, an Ohio lumber dealer with enough capital to start a steam-driven sawmill, they began to build a town on the lowland between forest and bay. They called it Seattle. They cut the forest on the western slope and dragged the logs to Yesler's mill. The land around the wharf they firmed up with sawdust and bark. When there wasn't enough waste, they began sluicing dirt from the hills.

Across the years the developers turned the topography of Seattle upside down. They spread the western hills over marsh and tideflat, buried the old waterfront and created a new one, covered half of the tidal area of the original bay with new land, and built Harbor Island, the largest manmade island in the world. They dug canals from the sound to Lake Union and from Lake Union to Lake Washington, lowering the lake itself, drying up its outlet, Black River, but giving the city a total of 193 miles of waterfront. They rebuilt Green Lake, making it smaller and deeper, capped springs, drove tunnels underneath the business district, and built a bed of roads and rails to ensnare the suburbs.

In the orgy of development much natural beauty disappeared. Townsfolk wrangled angrily over costs and benefits. The lakes became unsafe for swimming, the air polluted by the concentration of industry, and by the business community's determination to funnel all possible traffic through the downtown area. But the disease created its own antibodies. Activists emerged to fight for fresher air, cleaner water, easier access, and people-oriented neighborhoods. Out of the conflicts came a community which, when it found itself described in the 1970s as "America's most liveable city," was not so much appreciative of the compliment as wary about the consequences. The fate of the earlier occupants of this attractive land is a cautionary tale.

*From a tourist pamphlet; courtesy of
Photograph Collection, University of
Washington Library*

Chapter 1

THE OLD ORDER PASSETH

1850-1873

David Swinton Maynard, affectionately known as Doc Maynard, posed for this photo about 1865 in E. A. Sammis' studio. A generous man who gave away much of his property to help the city grow, Maynard was Seattle's first physician, first merchant, first commercial fish packer, first real estate dealer, first notary public, first court clerk, first court commissioner, first justice of the peace, first Indian agent, first man admitted to practice law, first person to open a hospital, and first to get a divorce. Photograph by E. A. Sammis; courtesy of Photograph Collection, University of Washington Library

The Indians were friendly. They were Coastal Salish, of the Duwamish and Suquamish peoples, and had lived for centuries near the mouths of the mountain streams emptying into the inland sea. Theirs was an economy of abundance. From the annual runs of salmon they could harvest in a few weeks enough food to last a year. The forest supplied wood for their houses and fibers for their clothing. They had plenty and were willing to share with the whites whose arrival gave them access to metal goods, firearms, cheap blankets, and exotic clothing as well as new diseases and new vices.

Even before the first white arrivals reached Puget Sound, the Duwamish and Suquamish had been struck by smallpox and malaria brought to the Northwest Coast by seaborne explorers and fur traders and carried by the Indians from tribe to tribe. Thus, their numbers were declining. The arrival of the settlers and white civilization added alcohol to their problems, yet they were friendly to the aliens on their land.

The Indians watched without protest as their visitors staked out claims along the shores their people had used so long that no one's memory ran to the contrary. They saw the houses of the whites rise, watched the growth of Henry Yesler's steam mill and the retreat of the forest, without protest.

Trouble came, however, with the treaty-making. The United States wanted the Indians to give up title to most of their land so it could be legally transferred to settlers. On January 22, 1855, Governor Isaac Stevens met with the Indians of the Northern Sound at a site the whites called Elliott Point and the Indians called Muchl-te-oh (good camping ground.) Stevens offered to let the Indians keep 48,000 acres divided among four reservations and to pay $15,000 in twenty equal annual installments in return for title to most of the present counties of King, Snohomish, Skagit, Whatcom, Island, and Kitsap.

Many Indian leaders spoke, most eloquently Chief Seattle, who had come to share the white belief that his people were a dying race, destined for oblivion. In sorrow they signed, though they still far outnumbered the whites on their land. But later that year, when Stevens was negotiating with the tribes east of the Cascades, the Yakimas rebelled.

The Indian war spread to the west side of the mountains when volunteer militiamen tried to

arrest Nisqually leaders they feared might make trouble. A band of Indians attacked outlying farms in the White River valley, killing several families and triggering a rush of refugees to Seattle and Steilacoom. Isaac L. Sterett, the naval commander in the area, warned the secretary of the navy that the situation was desperate: "The valor and prowess of the Indians have been greatly underrated, the forces now in the field and indeed the whole military resources of the Territory are totally inadequate to conduct the war with success or even to afford protection to the settlers."

At this time of crisis, Seattle and his people remained neutral, even friendly. They agreed to move to the reservation, though no payment had yet been made. In January of 1856 they warned the whites of an impending attack on the settlement of Seattle. Alerted, the whites beat back the assault, and the Indian war died down. The Elliott Point Treaty was finally ratified in 1860. The terms of payment were never fully met, but the whites had the land and kept it.

The Yesler Mill Cook House was built of hewn logs during the winter of 1852-1853. It stood on Commercial Street (First Avenue South) between Washington and Mill streets (Yesler Way.) Here, Seattle's first sermon was preached, its first trial held, its first public entertainment given. When the cook house was torn down in 1866, no log buildings remained in the business district. Courtesy of Photograph Collection, University of Washington Library

The Reverend David E. Blaine, the first Protestant minister assigned to Seattle, was sent by the Genesee Conference of the Methodist Episcopal church. He and his wife, Catherine, arrived at Alki Point on November 26, 1853. After holding service in a log mess hall, the minister crossed the bay to the new community and preached in Bachelors' Hall on Front Street between Cherry and Columbia until the Little White Church was completed at Second and Columbia in May of 1855.

Kate Blaine opened Seattle's first school in Bachelors' Hall in the spring of 1854, teaching a class of thirteen girls and one boy. The school closed when the Blaines were transferred to Oregon after the Indian war of 1855-1856. A plaque marks the site on First Avenue. Courtesy of Photograph Collection, University of Washington Library

Harry Smith, a physician and poet, was one of the first Seattle residents to speak Duwamish. He was present at the negotiation of the Point Elliott Treaty in 1855 and took notes on the moving reply made by Chief Seattle to Territorial Governor Isaac Stevens' oratory. Years later, Smith wrote out a flowery translation from his original notes: Photograph by Asahel Curtis; courtesy of Photograph Collection, University of Washington Library

On August 4, 1853, Doc Maynard sold Block Four of his property to Captain Leonard Felker for $350. Felker spent another $450 to put up a handsome frame building which served as the first Seattle home of many pioneer families, including those of A. C. Anderson, Bailey Gatzert, John Leary, and M. R. Maddocks. The Felker House, north of First Avenue on the south side of Jackson Street, was for some years managed by a redoubtable woman known variously as Mary Ann Boyer, Mary Ann Conklin, and, because of her exceptionally salty language, Old Mother Damnable and Madame Damnable. Felker sold the property to A. C. Anderson in 1861 for $2,000, and Anderson disposed of it twenty years later for $51,000. The building was destroyed in the great fire of 1889. Courtesy of Photograph Collection, University of Washington Library

"Every part of this country is sacred to my people. Every hillside, every valley, every plain and grove has been hallowed by some fond memory or some sad experience of my tribe. Even the rocks, which seem to lie dumb as they swelter in the sun along the silent sea shore in solemn grandeur thrill with memories of past events connected with the lives of my people; the very dust under your feet responds more lovingly to our footsteps than to yours, because it is the ashes of our ancestors, and our bare feet are conscious of the sympathetic touch, for the soil is rich with the life of our kindred.

"The noble braves, fond mothers, glad, happy-hearted maidens, and even the little children, who lived and rejoiced here for a brief season, and whose very names are not forgotten, still love these sombre solitudes, and their deep fastnesses which at even-tide grow shadowy with the presence of dusky spirits.

"When the Red Man shall have perished from this earth and the memory of my tribe shall have become a myth among the White Men these shores will swarm with the invisible dead of my tribe and when your children's children think themselves alone in the field, the store, the shop, upon the highway, or in the silence of the pathless woods, they will not be alone. In all the earth there is no place dedicated to solitude. At night when the streets of your cities and villages are silent and you think them deserted, they will throng with the returning hosts that once filled and still love this beautiful land. The White Man will never be alone.

"Let him be just and deal kindly with my people, for the dead are not powerless.

"Dead—did I say? There is no death. Only a change of worlds!"

*. . . closing words of Chief Seattle's oration
Point Elliott treaty grounds
January 23, 1855*

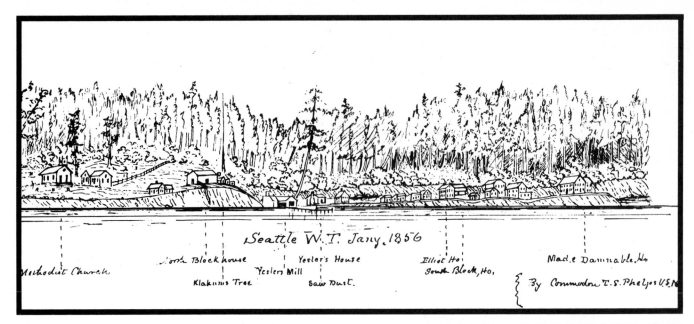

Seattle W.T. Jany. 1856

Methodist Church   North Blockhouse   Yesler's House   Elliot Ho   Mad.e Damnable. Ho
                    Klakums Tree   Yesler Mill   Saw Dust.   South Block. Ho,   By Commodore T. S. Phelps U.S.N

Thomas Stowell Phelps was a thirty-year-old lieutenant on the sloop-of-war Decatur *when Indians attacked Seattle. His sketch of the settlement as seen from the bay shows the straggle of buildings between today's Fourth Avenue and the bluff at First Avenue and is far more believable than his account of the skirmish published in* United Service *magazine in December 1881. Courtesy of Photograph Collection, University of Washington Library*

Seattle at the time of the battle. From a sketch by Lieutenant Phelps, with added identifications by Paul Dorpat; courtesy of Photograph Collection, University of Washington Library

PLAN OF SEATTLE
1855-6   FROM LT. THOMAS S. PHELPS NAVIGATOR ON THE DECATUR

A. NORTH BLOCKHOUSE
B. MRS. HOLGATES
C. YESLER'S MILL
D. YESLER'S HOUSE
E. MADAM DAMNABLE
F. PLUMMER'S HOUSE
G. HOWITZER
H. SOUTH BLOCKHOUSE
I. TOMPEPPER'S HOUSE
J. YESLER'S WHARF
K. BARRICADES

FIRST (OR FRONT ST.)
CHERRY
ELLIOT BAY
U.S.S. DECATUR
BARK BRONTES
FIRST
(Mill St. or) YESLER
WASHINGTON
COMMERCIAL ST. (NOW FIRST S.)
MAIN
JACKSON
KING
TIDE MARSH
C SAND SPIT
TIDEFLATS

When the Indian attack began, women and children took refuge in the blockhouses. Catherine Blaine, wife of the Methodist minister, had just had a baby; she was carried to safety in a rocking chair. Louisa Denny, though about to give birth, walked to the blockhouse carrying her youngest child and an apronful of hot biscuits. Three-year-old Emily Inez Denny, who years later painted this picture, toddled along. She retained one vivid memory of the incident:

A shot was accidentally fired from a gun inside the fort [and] a pale-faced, dark-haired lady narrowly escaped death. The bullet passed through a loop of her hair, below the ear, just beside the white neck. Her hair was dressed in an old-fashioned way, parted in the middle of the forehead and smoothly brushed down over the ears, divided and twisted on each side, and the two ropes of hair coiled together at the back of her head. Like a flashlight photograph her face is imprinted on my memory; nothing before it or afterward for some time can I claim to recall.

Original painting on display at Seattle Museum of History and Industry; courtesy of Photograph Collection, University of Washington Library

*Chief Seattle was photographed by
E. M. Sammis in 1864.*

*Four years after the Indian war,
the Duwamish and Suquamish who had
given up their lands had not been paid.
The Senate had not even ratified the
Elliott Point Treaty. At a meeting with
Indian Agent Michael T. Simmons at
Port Madison, the aging Seattle spoke
again:*

*I want you to understand
what I say. I do not drink rum,
and always advise our people not
to do so. I am not a bad man. I
am always and have always been
a friend of the whites, Mr.
Simmons. Why doesn't our paper
come back to us? You always say
you hope it will come soon, but it
does not come. I fear we are
forgotten and that we are all to be
cheated out of our lands. I have
been very poor and hungry all
winter and am sick now. In a
little while I will die. I should like
to be paid for my lands, before I
die. Many of my people died
during the cold winter without
getting their pay. When I die my
people will be very poor. They will
get no property, no chief, no one to
talk for them....Indians are not
bad. Mean white people are bad to
us. If any person says we do not
want our paper [treaty] he lies.
You see I am very sick. I want
you to write quickly to your great
chief what I say. I am done.*

*The Senate ratified the treaty in
1860, but three more years passed before
the first payment was made. Chief Seattle
died in January 1866. Courtesy of
Photograph Collection, University of
Washington Library*

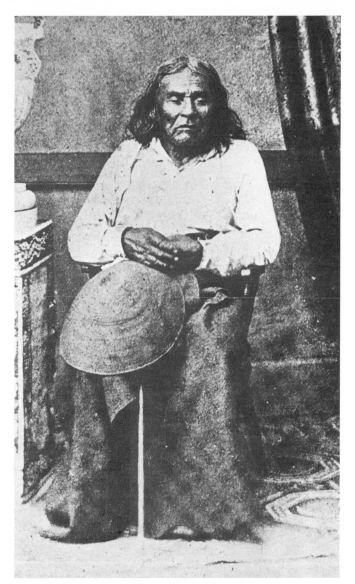

*In 1860 Sarah Yesler posed on the porch of
the Yesler House on Front Street for what
is thought to be the first picture taken in
Seattle. The water flume was removed the
following year.*

*The fenced-in home of Harry Smith
is on the right, the Hillory Butler house
is directly behind Yesler's, and Captain
S. D. Libby's house is on the hill behind
Butler's. The small house behind and to
the left of Yesler's is that of L. V.
Wyckoff, later sheriff. The edge of the
forest is today's Third Avenue. Yesler's
maples, which later bore the sour fruit
of Seattle's first lynching, had just been
planted to the right of the house and
were fenced off from horses and deer.
Photograph by E. A. Clark; courtesy of
Photograph Collection, University of
Washington Library*

In the scramble for government payrolls, which was a preoccupation of the pioneers, Seattle lost the territorial capitol to Olympia but won the territorial university. Arthur Denny, as a legislator, drew up the bill which in January 1861 located the school in Seattle. Then Denny, as a Seattle promoter, donated most of the ten-acre tract on which it was built.

The legislature had set a deadline of one year for the school to be in operation. The townsfolk joined to help clear, grub, fence, and plant Denny's knoll to wheat and blue grass. Then they rushed through the construction of a two-story school building, a boarding house, and a forty-foot-by-fifty-foot presidential mansion (seen at left) for a total cost of $30,787. The legislature accepted it as complete on December 31, 1861.

Territorial school superintendent B. C. Lippincott, who thought grade schools and high schools should come first, complained that "there is not a young man in the Territory who could pass an examination to enter the University.

There is not in all King County one hundred children of lawful age to attend even a district school. Where is the propriety of spending all this money?" He was right about the paucity of scholars. The university did not graduate anyone until 1876, when Clara A. McCarty of Puyallup received a bachelor of science diploma. But Seattle had its university when the time came. Photograph by E. M. Sammis, circa 1865; courtesy of Seattle Public Library

Lucy Whipple Carr came to Oregon with her husband in 1858 and then to Seattle in 1861. He helped build the Territorial University while she taught a class of about thirty children in the building during the summer of 1862, thus becoming the first public school-marm. (Mrs. Blaine's class was by private subscription.) The Carrs moved to Oregon, but returned to Seattle in 1877 when he was named deputy postmaster. They had been born in the same month in 1832 and died five weeks apart in 1912. Courtesy of Photograph Collection, University of Washington Library

Asa Shinn Mercer arrived in Seattle in 1861, a year after he was graduated from Franklin College in Ohio. He found a job helping to lay the foundation for the Territorial University building. A year later the Reverend David Bagley, president of the board of commissioners, determined that Mercer was "thorough in discipline and high-toned morality" and hired him to serve as acting president and to be the entire faculty during the school's first two eleven-week semesters.

The young president said later: Previous to opening school, I spent three weeks, hiring two Indians with a canoe, and traveled about 400 miles, visiting every logging camp on the east side of Puget Sound from Bellingham Bay to Olympia, trying to induce any young men whom I might find engaged in the logging camps to come to Seattle and enter school; succeeded in getting about one dozen, varying in age from twenty to twenty-five years. In order to secure them, I agreed to pay them $1.50 a cord for wood chopped from down timber in front of the university grounds....I contracted with Captain Finch of the steamer Eliza Anderson, the only passenger steamer at the time plying on Puget Sound, to supply him with cordwood, getting $2.50 a cord. H. L. Yesler, who owned the wharf, gave me the free use of the wharf, thus saving me 25¢ a cord. There were but two horse teams in the city at the time, and I had to pay $1 a cord for having the wood hauled to the wharf.... The young men being expert handlers of the axe averaged two cords each Saturday (History of King County by Clarence Bagley). Courtesy of Photograph Collection, University of Washington Library

E. M. Sammis, who opened the first photographic studio in Seattle, was at Plummer's Hall on the southwest corner of Main Street when he made this photograph looking up Commercial Street (First Avenue South) in 1865.

Smoke rises from the stack of Yesler's mill just behind and to the left of the flagpole. The tree line has retreated to about Fifth Avenue. The

Territorial University dominates the hill. The Little White Church (Methodist), the dark, two-story Masonic Hall, and the big white Occidental Hotel are the most conspicuous buildings. The fences were needed to protect gardens from horses, pigs, and deer. Courtesy of Photograph Collection, University of Washington Library

The national census of 1860 showed King County to have 220 males and eighty-two females, and most of the women were married. This frustrating proportion did not change greatly for several years. In 1864 Asa Mercer went back East and, to the delight of the Seattle citizenry, persuaded eleven young women (and two men) to accompany him to Puget Sound. A reception was held at the university at which the young ladies (one was only sixteen, another seventeen, and the others between eighteen and twenty) were introduced.

So great was the enthusiasm that the self-styled Female Emigrant Agent was encouraged to return East with funds provided by local bachelors and to recruit hundreds more potential schoolteachers and brides. But Mercer's plans went awry. He was looked on as little better than a pimp by Eastern editors, he was hornswoggled in his negotiations for a steamship, and eleven of the matrimonially minded migrants stayed in San Francisco—along with the ship. The rest of the party made it north on lumber schooners, their arrival spaced across several weeks. About thirty unmarried women reached the town and all but one disappeared into matrimony and myth as the Mercer Girls. Drawing from Harper's Weekly, January 1866; courtesy of Photograph Collection, University of Washington Library

Mercer Girl ticket. Courtesy of Photograph Collection, University of Washington Library

Erected in 1865 at Commercial and Mill streets (now First and Yesler), this building housed not only Pinkham's Variety Store and the Kelloggs' Drug Store but, on the second floor, the studio of Seattle's first photographer. The large square on the roof is Sammis' solar printer. Photograph by E. M. Sammis, 1865; Courtesy of Photograph Collection, University of Washington Library

William "Billy" Fife, who painted this stylized interpretation of Seattle in 1872, was born in Cape Town, South Africa, and came to the United States about 1856. According to an obituary in the Weekly Pacific Tribune when he died March 17, 1876: "His works are on almost every steamer on Puget Sound, and in most of the public houses of Seattle." The only one known to have survived, this painting is in the collection of the late Robert Hitchman, president of the Washington State Historical Society. Courtesy of Photograph Collection, University of Washington Library

During the boom in hop exports, between 1882 when a blight struck the European hop fields and 1887 when the hop louse attacked the plants in Western Washington, Indians did most of the picking. Canoes on their way to the White River and Puyallup Valley farms often paused at the west end of Vine, Cedar, and Broad streets. This canoe landing has since been covered by four lines of railroad track, wharves, warehouses, shops, and streets. Courtesy of Seattle Public Library

THE RAILROAD YEARS

1873-1893

Western — —graph Company.

The rules of this Company require that all messages received for transmission, shall be written on the message blanks of the Company, under and subject to the conditions printed thereon, which conditions have been agreed to, by the sender of the following message.
JAS. GAMBLE, General Sup't, }
SAN FRANCISCO. }
WILLIAM ORTON, President, } New York.
G. H. MUMFORD, Secretary, }

Kalama 14 July 1873

Received at Seattle 14 July 1873 140P M.

To Hon A A Denny

We have located Terminus on Commencement Bay

R R Rice
J C Ainsworth
Commissioners

11 pass 298
H Kaw

On July 2, 1864, Abraham Lincoln signed a bill granting a charter to the Northern Pacific for a railroad connecting the western rim of Lake Superior with Puget Sound.

From the start of American settlement, pioneers on the Sound anticipated the coming of rails that would end their isolation from the States. Now, the great day seemed near. Every hamlet on salt water caught the terminus disease. Homesteaders lifted their eyes unto the hills through which they expected track to be laid. When not watching the mountain passes in anticipation of survey crews, they kept a suspicious eye on neighboring communities lest they manage to mislead the transportation folk back East with false claims of their own terminal merit.

The contest did not end when the Northern Pacific's selection committee wired Arthur Denny on July 14, 1873, to say Tacoma would be the western terminus. Seattle enthusiasts tried to build a line through the Cascades with their own money and muscle. Although the city could not complete the line, it obtained rights-of-way that later proved useful in obtaining rail service.

Financial difficulties delayed completion of the Northern Pacific main line until 1883. Five more years went by before track was laid through the Cascade Mountains, permitting traffic to bypass rival Portland and giving Puget Sound ports an equal chance at transcontinental shipments.

Even during the years when Tacoma had railroad service and Seattle did not, Seattle maintained a population edge over the terminus city. Its central location on the sound, which made it the nesting place for the mosquito fleet—the flotilla of small steamers that carried freight and passengers between the salt water communities—kept Seattle competitive in the race for trade and population.

Seattle helped its cause by earning a reputation for law and order during the anti-Chinese violence that swept Washington in the 1880s. Chinese work gangs, imported from Canton Province and hired out by local Chinese contractors, did much of the railroad construction in the far West. When the transcontinental lines were in place and Chinese began competing with white labor for other jobs, they were bitterly resented. Economic fear bred racial hatred. Congress responded with a law excluding the entry of Chinese laborers, but white agitators demanded the expulsion of Chinese already here.

In November, 1885, a well-organized mob in Tacoma, encouraged by the mayor and abetted by the sheriff, drove out the entire Chinese community and burned their houses. The arrival of federal troops prevented a similar occurrence in Seattle at the time. Two months later the anti-Chinese in Seattle surprised authorities by herding 350 Chinese onto the *Queen of the Pacific* for deportation to San Francisco.

Territorial Chief Justice Roger Greene directed a writ of habeas corpus to the captain of the steamer, demanding that any Chinese who wished to stay be put ashore. The Home Guards, a local militia, took control of the dock and escorted the Chinese back to their homes. The next day, amid renewed agitation, fighting broke out at the corner of First Avenue and Mill Street (Yesler Way). An anti-Chinese Canadian was killed and four others wounded when the Home Guard opened fire.

The anti-Chinese secured warrants for the arrest of five leading citizens, including Judge Thomas Burke, on charges they had illegally brought about the shooting. Governor Watson Squire declared martial law so the warrants could

The existence of coal in the Cascade foothills east of Seattle had been known since Seattle was founded, but not until 1871 was it considered profitable to mine it. Then the Seattle Coal and Transportation Company solicited work-help from the community. Nearly all able-bodied males in town helped smooth a path down which the black gold could flow to the sound. A tramway was built to carry coal cars from the

mine at Newcastle to Lake Washington. The coal cars were barged to Union Bay, hauled across the Portage to Lake Union, barged to the south end of the lake, and run on rails to bunkers at the foot of Pine Street.

In 1872 Seattle Coal and Transportation was purchased by Charles D. Shattuck and S. Dinsmore of San Francisco. They imported Puget Sound's first locomotive to pull the coal

cars back and forth between Lake Union and the bunkers. Seattle declared a holiday on March 26, 1872, and the company gave free rides all day when, as the Intelligencer *put it, "the first locomotive that ever shuttled and snorted and dashed through the dense forest surrounding the waters of Puget Sound" began service. Courtesy of Seattle Public Library*

not be served. Federal troops arrived the next day. Burke and the others of the Home Guard were never indicted. Many Chinese left, but those not intimidated were allowed to remain. Unlike Tacoma, Seattle emerged from the conflict with a reputation for protecting the rights of minority citizens, a reputation that served it well in the competition for trade with the Orient.

Seattle was even able to turn the great fire of 1889 to its benefit. Though the conflagration destroyed many cherished buildings—a few of them handsome—and left thousands temporarily homeless, it permitted reconstruction of the business district and the waterfront on a less haphazard basis. When James J. Hill, "the empire builder," at last brought the Great Northern to salt water at Seattle in 1893, the flourishing city of some 50,000 seemed poised for a boom.

The black building in the center is the house of William N. Bell. It stood on the northwest corner of Second Avenue and Cherry, where the eighteen-story Hoge Building was erected in 1911. The site was originally claimed by C. D. Boren, who built a cabin which was burned in the Indian war. He sold the lot to Bell in 1855. The picture is believed to date from the winter of 1869. Courtesy of Seattle Public Library

"On Thursday evening, in Pumphrey & Young's Bookstore on Commercial Street, we were shown a fine painting of this city from the hill back of town, which, on inquiry, we learned was executed by Harrison Eastman, Esq., the well-known artist of San Francisco, who is at present temporarily stopping here. The town is spread out before the spectator as on a map, embracing the business portion, the private residences with their neat gardens, and the harbor in front, dotted with numerous white sails, and Freeport (West Seattle) and the snow-capped Olympic Mountains in the distance. It is a beautiful picture, and Mr. Eastman richly deserves the thanks of this community for the care he has taken in its preparation" (The Intelligencer, May 30, 1874).

Painting by Harrison Eastman, New York Public Library photograph; courtesy of Photograph Collection, University of Washington Library

The Occidental Hotel at Front Street (First Avenue) and James was built in 1865 by John Condon and M. R. Maddocks. It could accommodate about thirty guests. It was purchased by John Collins, and in 1883 he converted it to a four-story brick building covering the entire block. Leased to the Seattle Hotel Company (J. D. Lowman, George H. Heilbron, and A. B. Stewart) in 1887, it was destroyed two years later in the great fire. Taken in 1872 from the intersection of Occidental and Main streets, the picture shows Mrs. Frances Guye's boarding house on the right of the Occidental, with A. Slorak's Saloon occupying the building and shed to the left. Courtesy of Photograph Collection, University of Washington Library

The plume of smoke from the Yesler Mill in this 1871 stereo view by George Moore indicates more pollution than profit. The mill was small and outdated. Yesler had dropped out of the cargo (waterborne) trade and was selling lumber almost exclusively to the local market, which was depressed.

Mill Street (Yesler Way) was composed largely of refuse from the mill, chiefly sawdust. The stores, reading from the right, were: L. Reinig's Seattle Bakery, M. A. Kelly's Pioneer Drug Store, Waddell and Miles' Stove Store, F. V. Snyder's City Market, and the Cooms and Pumphrey Book & Stationery Store. Courtesy of Photograph Collection, University of Washington Library

Obsessed with the need to establish a direct trade route through the Cascades, the Seattle delegation worked a bill through the territorial legislature authorizing lotteries on condition that the sponsor pay 10 percent of gross receipts to King County to help pay for a road through Snoqualmie Pass.

Henry Yesler (top left) was among those who saw in the legislation a way out of the financial problems posed by the Panic of '73. He offered his mill, which was famous but outdated, as first prize in a drawing for which he proposed to sell 60,000 tickets at $5 each.

Like the less imaginative statewide lottery authorized by the 1982 legislature, Yesler's brainchild ended up in court. The operators of other gambling enterprises and the Respectable Element ganged up on Yesler, bringing suit to block the lottery. The Territorial Supreme Court declared it unconstitutional, the post office refused to deliver mail addressed to Yesler, and the district attorney charged him with conducting an illegal gambling operation. Yesler was found guilty and fined $25. Nobody got back money from the tickets that had been sold.

The land Yesler tried to give away as prizes multiplied in value in later years. When he died in 1892, his estate included $1,098,580 in real estate and $47,654 in personal property. From History of Seattle *by Frederick Grant; courtesy of Photograph Collection, University of Washington Library*

The Intelligencer *building, on the west side of First Avenue south of Cherry, was built in 1874 by Henry Yesler, who rented it to S. L. Maxwell, one of the men on the porch. The man in front of the second story window is Isaac M. Hall, an attorney. The town council met in Hall's office in 1876. When the* Intelligencer *moved to new offices in 1875, the print shop was occupied by Boyd, Poncin & Young, purveyors of dry goods. Photograph by George Moore, from a stereoptican view; courtesy of Photograph Collection, University of Washington Library*

Built in Portland in 1858 and brought immediately to the sound, the Eliza Anderson was the first luxury steamer on local waters. She served first on the mail run between Olympia and Victoria. Fares started at $20 a head for passengers, $15 a head for cattle. With the arrival of competition they dropped, for humans, to as low as 50¢ from Olympia to Victoria with a free meal thrown in.

Among the ship's charms was a steam calliope, purchased from a bankrupt circus, with which the captain serenaded passengers and shore dwellers and exasperated the British community in Victoria with Fourth of July renditions of "Yankee Doodle" and "The Stars and Stripes Forever." Maritime historian Gordon Newell tells in Totem Tales of Old Seattle of the time when the Eliza Anderson was caught carrying too heavy a load through Deception Pass. In the freight were seven pianos, eight head of cattle, and a dozen barrels of whisky. With the ship taking on water fast, the skipper opened the pilot house window and roared, "Overboard with the cattle." Into the water they went. "Overboard with the pianos." Thus lightened, the Eliza Anderson limped into Seattle. When the company agent came aboard he asked, "Cap, don't you think you acted a little hasty in getting those pianos overboard before the whisky?"

"Hell, man," roared the skipper, "you can't drink pianos."

In 1897, after nearly forty years of service on the Sound, the old Anderson started for the Yukon River with a payload of would-be prospectors. She made it as far as Dutch Harbor in the Aleutians before breaking down for the last time. Photograph from University of Washington Library; print courtesy of Argus Magazine

The Alida, launched in Olympia in 1869 and rebuilt in Seattle the following year, was a trim little sidewheeler with a dozen comfortable staterooms, but she was seldom a moneymaker. Too unstable for safe operation on the Strait of Juan de Fuca, she was taken off the Olympia-Seattle-Victoria run. For a time she towed coal barges. At another period she had the mail contract but lost it to a faster vessel. Briefly, she worked as a ferry running between Old Tacoma and the Northern Pacific wharf in New Tacoma. She was turned into a floating pest house during a smallpox epidemic, and finally, while beached in Gig Harbor in 1890, she was destroyed in a forest fire.

Here, the Alida is docked north of Columbia Street, where Western Avenue now traverses fill land. The sawlogs of the Yesler mill are in the foreground and the large buildings, left to right, are: the Methodist Protestant Church, the Territorial University, and the new Central School. The large house at right center is the Shoudy residence on the northwest corner of Second and Marion. Courtesy of Photograph Collection, University of Washington Library

The sidewheeler George E. Starr, shown under construction in the Hammond shipyard at the foot of Cherry Street, was launched in 1879. Though she ended her career as a coal barge, for a decade the Starr was considered the best vessel in her class on the sound. Captain William Hammond's decision in 1869 to move his shipbuilding business to Seattle from Port Ludlow was a sign of the increasing centralization of marine traffic on Elliott Bay. Courtesy of Photograph Collection, University of Washington Library

The bark Windward, outward bound from Seattle in December of 1875 with a cargo of lumber, was driven ashore at Useless Bay on the south side of Whidbey Island. J. M. Colman bought the wreck and had it towed to Seattle, where the lumber was off-loaded and the vessel stripped of sails, copper, and furnishings. The hulk lay for years in the tidewash below the bluff at the foot of Marion Street, a favorite platform for divers. When the restructuring of the waterfront began, the Windward was buried under dirt sluiced from Denny Hill. It lies now beneath the Colman Building annex at Marion and Western Avenue, well in from the waterfront. Photograph by Peterson and Brother; courtesy of Photograph Collection, University of Washington Library

The Seattle and Walla Walla Railroad was incorporated in 1873 immediately after Seattle learned of the Northern Pacific's selection of Tacoma as its terminus. The townsfolk set out to lay track over the mountains to the Inland Empire but quickly ran out of energy and money. In 1877 S&WW managed to reach Renton, and that was far enough. There was coal in the Renton area (the first discovery was in the hills at the end of Williams Street), and the railroad poured it into the bunkers of Seattle's waterfront, attracting colliers serving San Francisco and steamers needing fuel. When the line opened, the locomotive Arthur A. Denny, named after the S&WW president, hauled passengers between the towns, free, in cars that had been built in Seattle. Courtesy of Seattle Public Library

A. W. Piper, a Seattle baker, strolls the boardwalk on Front Street with his son Wallis and their dog Jack in 1879. Beacon Hill, still unlogged, looms in the background. Barely visible in the extreme right corner is the post supporting the upstairs porch of the Pontius Building, in which the great Seattle fire began ten years later.

The tide still lapped the cliff below Front Street (First Avenue) and the Pontius Building, like the neighboring Woodward Grain Warehouse, which housed the Occidental Brotherhood and Peter's Furs, Cigars and Liquors, rested on pilings. The third floor and roof of the Arlington Hotel can be seen just to the left of the granary roof. The white buildings farther down Front house the Northern Pacific Brewery at the foot of Columbia Street. Photograph by Peterson and Brother; courtesy of Photograph Collection, University of Washington Library

This 1878 photo shows the same stretch of Front Street, seen here from the water. The Pontius Building is at the extreme left, the granary left center. The bluff below Front has been faced with logs, and shacks on pilings have sprouted from the tideflats.

The numbered buildings are (1) Congregational Church; (2) Territorial University; (3) Central School; (4) Presbyterian Church; (5) Methodist Church; (6) the residence of Dr. G. A Weed, who later served as mayor; and (7) property belonging to Hattie Greene, whose residence is over the lip of the hill. Photograph by Peterson and Brother; courtesy of Photograph Collection, University of Washington Library

The photo of the Pipers was taken from the window of the two-story white building (7), left center in this picture. The building was occupied by the M. R. Maddocks Drug Store. Directly across Front Street from it can be seen the raised porch of the Pontius Building, which seems to be attached to the Woodward Granary, but isn't. The Elephant Store sold general goods and groceries but no elephants. The next three buildings were owned by George Frye, and building (4) belonged to George Roper. The dark building with the white false front (5) and the slant roof building next to it (6) were the Williamson Foundry. The large white house beyond the tall, dark evergreen (9) was the A. A. Denny residence. Photograph by Peterson and Brother; courtesy of Photograph Collection, University of Washington Library

The year 1880 opened bleakly. Seattle's greatest blizzard began on January 6. Thirty-one inches of snow fell the first day, sixty-four before the skies cleared. The Hunt and McDonald blacksmith shop and the Williams and Cooper boiler shop collapsed; all over town, woodsheds, outbuildings, and wooden awnings fell. The telegraph lines went down, and Seattle was cut off from communication with Portland until January 21. The town council even appropriated $100 for street clearing. During the year snowfall totalled 102 inches. Photograph by Peterson and Brother; courtesy of Photograph Collection, University of Washington Library

Yesler's Pavilion, at the corner of Front and Cherry, was built for the 1865 Fourth of July celebration. For two decades it was the most popular, almost the inevitable, scene for theatricals, concerts, and speeches. Susan B. Anthony, Elizabeth Cady Stanton, and Abigail Scott Duniway spoke for woman suffrage; Yankee Plummer gave an entertainment; S. S. Fowler expounded on the science of phrenology; John L. Sullivan sparred; and Madam Anna Bishop, when seventy years of age, drew from all parts of the sound an audience which paid the extraordinary price of five dollars a ticket to hear her sing.

Behind the pavilion is the home of Sheriff Lewis V. Wyckoff. Farther up the hill are the First Baptist Church, the J. George residence, and the Condon residence. The white house at the crest of the hill on the north (left) side belonged to C. Anderson. The Dexter Horton Building now stands where the line of shade trees can be seen, and the Hoge Building is now where the Spring Beds sign advertises an emporium operated by Schillestad—Upholsterer and Undertaker. Courtesy of Seattle Public Library

40

Mourners gathered before the Occidental Hotel in bright mid-afternoon sunlight on September 26, 1881, to pay tribute to President James Abram Garfield, who died September 19, two months after being shot by a disappointed office seeker. Judge Orange Jacobs, who had served in Congress with Garfield, delivered the eulogy, which included the following flight:

As the sun of the physical world, the brightest and grandest of all the luminaries of the firmament, sinks to rest, tingeing the clouds that stretch along the horizon with golden glories of its declining rays, so Garfield, the sun-intellect of this nation, has gone to his repose, reflecting the light of his noble deeds and unfaltering patriotism, tingeing the breaking clouds of dissention with the beauty and effulgence of hope and peace.

Trinity Church and Rectory stand behind the hotel. Note the growth of the Yesler maples, at left. Photograph by Peterson and Brother; courtesy of Photograph Collection, University of Washington Library

On October 13, 1881, a policeman *"of good family, mild, gentle and charitable,"* according to his obituary, was fatally wounded by Benjamin Payne, whose disorderly conduct had caused public complaint. Payne was jailed pending trial.

On January 17, 1882, a grocery clerk, recently married, was shot dead near Third and Marion by two robbers. A citizens' posse found James Sullivan and William Howard hiding under a pile of hay on the Harrington and Smith wharf. One had a revolver with an empty chamber, the other had a number of cartridges that fitted the gun.

The following morning Justice of the Peace Samuel Coombs conducted a hearing in Yesler Hall. After testimony from twenty-eight witnesses he bound the pair over for trial. Immediately the crowd overpowered the police and sheriff's deputies to carry the men out onto James Street, to the trees Yesler had planted in 1860. A timber was thrust between the forks of two maples and ropes were thrown over it. The men were hanged.

The mob then went to the jail, got Payne and hanged him too, though Roger Sherman Greene, chief justice of the territorial supreme court, had to be restrained from cutting the rope with a pocket knife. From Harper's Weekly, February 4, 1882; courtesy of Photograph Collection, University of Washington Library

The intersection of James Street with Mill Street (Yesler Way) at Front Street (First Avenue). The Occidental hotel is on the left. The Vanity Fair Saloon and Franch Grocery are across Yesler. The masonry building is the Mackintock & Reeves bank. The white building is the Gem Saloon. The Kellogg Drug Store is on the ground floor of the building dead center. Yesler Hall, on the second floor, was reached by stairs concealed behind the maples. The Daily Post is in the right corner. Courtesy of Seattle Public Library

The Post Building, at Post and Mill streets, was built by John Leary in 1882 for $30,000 and for several years was considered Seattle's most fashionable business address. It housed the Post-Intelligencer, which had been formed by the consolidation of the Daily and Weekly Post *and the* Daily and Weekly Intelligencer *in October 1881. Other occupants included Lowman & Hanford Stationers, the Llewellyn & Co. real estate office, a brokerage house, an attorney, and the post office.

The men here are awaiting the arrival of mail, often a frustrating experience since the Northern Pacific contrived to delay Seattle-bound mail in Tacoma for as much as twenty-two hours. Courtesy of Seattle Public Library

The principal water supply for Seattle in the early 1880s was the Charles Coppin Waterworks at the southeast corner of Ninth and Columbia. The windmill atop the Coppin residence drew water into the tower tank. Courtesy of Photograph Collection, University of Washington Library

Maple's Hall in the White River Valley was a typical community center of the day: a false-front building with a general store on its ground floor, idlers on its porch, and a second-story meeting room open to all groups and promising "universal mental liberty."

The man seated by the door in this circa 1882 photograph is Jacob W. Maple, who settled on the Duwamish in 1851. Standing by him in the doorway is the store owner, T. W. Thornton. The little dog at Maple's feet was poisoned not long afterwards on the same night that a child was born to Mrs. Maple. The family had a saying, "We lost a dog but gained a daughter." Courtesy of Seattle Public Library

C. E. Watkins stood near the corner of Third and Stewart looking north across Belltown toward Magnolia when he took this picture in 1882. This is the view one would have had from the Denny Hotel, which was built later. The small wharf belonged to G. L. Mannings. The house with the oddly shaped roof in the left corner belonged to John Nation and was later occupied by Dr. O. G. Root. The two-story house with the large windows stood at Second and Lenora. It was the residence of School Superintendent E. S. Ingraham, who that year divided classrooms by grades. Asahel Curtis copy of a C. E. Watkins photograph, courtesy of Photograph Collection, University of Washington Library

In 1881 control of the Northern Pacific passed from the Philadelphia group that favored Tacoma to Henry Villard and associates. Though Villard had large investments in Portland, Seattle regarded him as friendly, especially when he purchased the old Seattle and Walla Walla short line for $350,000, renamed it the Columbia and Puget Sound, and began building south. Villard also made a $750,000 investment in western Washington coal fields, and the Oregon Improvement Company, which he controlled, assigned four steam colliers to carry coal from Seattle to San Francisco. Coal surpassed lumber as Seattle's main export, and the waterfront was reshaped with trestles and wharves reaching out to deep water.

The Talbot Coal Yard stood at the head of the Crawford & Harrington wharf. The big paddlewheel steamer at the Yesler Wharf is the S.S. Dakota. The old J. B. Libby is tied up farther in. Photograph by Theodore Peiser; courtesy of Photograph Collection, University of Washington Library

*"Where the iron of rail lets coal set sail,"
said an Oregon Improvement Company
pamphlet portraying the bunkers on the
Seattle waterfront. The ships carried the
coal to California. Courtesy of Seattle
Public Library*

*Henry Villard completed the main line
of the Northern Pacific in September of
1883, ten years behind schedule. Work
was finished simultaneously on the spur
connecting Portland with Tacoma by
way of Kalama on the Columbia River.
Puget Sound was now connected with
the Mississippi and Great Lakes.
Though Seattle still was not served by
the Northern Pacific, Villard promised
it would be.*

*When the railroad president visited
town on the steamer* Queen of the
Pacific *on September 14, every steamer
in the mosquito fleet, which served the
citizenry as a substitute for highways,
turned out to escort him to the dock.
The aquatic parade included the* Oliver
Wolcott, Eliza Anderson, Yakima,
Favorite, Messenger, Edna, Lucy, Lily,
Tillie, Arrow, Lone Fisherman, Queen
City, *and* Augusta.

*Buildings were adorned with
evergreen branches, banners, and flags.
Church bells rang and bands serenaded
the Villard party as a procession of
carriages took them on tour of the
would-be metropolis. The parade ended
at the Territorial University, which can
be seen dimly through the smoke as
Indian chefs grill salmon cut in the
traditional butterfly filet and spread on
sticks before an alder fire. It was the
town's greatest party, but Villard lost
control of the Northern Pacific before
the blandishments could bring Seattle
much benefit. Photograph by Theodore
Peiser; courtesy of Photograph
Collection University of Washington
Library*

The Arlington House showed the visitor, Villard, the changes that had arrived even without a railroad. Courtesy of Washington State Library

The City of Kingston *takes on coal at the Pacific Coast Coal Company wharf and bunker. The period must be the 1880s, for the Kingston was launched in 1884 and wrecked in 1889. West*

Seattle, seen in the background, was originally called Freeport when J. R. Williamson and others built a saw mill there in 1863-1864. The name was changed to Milton by E. L. Marshall in

the 1870s and then to West Seattle by the West Seattle Land and Improvement Company in the 1880s. Courtesy of Seattle Public Library

Mrs. C. W. Parkevin took this picture of Seattle's first public transportation, a stagecoach, in 1888 with one of the first Kodaks. According to Asahel Curtis, who made a copy from the original print, the coach ran from Commercial Street (First Avenue South) up First Hill to a turnaround in the woods about where Harvard Avenue is today. Fare was ten cents, one-way. The date service started is uncertain, but the line was discontinued on March 28, 1890, when the Yesler-Madison line was opened. Courtesy of Photograph Collection, University of Washington Library

A black man, George Washington, seen at the front of the car, drove Seattle's first streetcar on September 23, 1884. F. H. Osgood, manager and chief owner of the Seattle & Front Street line, is standing by the horses. E. B. Downing bulks large on the back step. Mrs. Osgood, Mrs. Struve, Mrs. Harrington, Mayor John Leary, and the city council are among those seated inside. Two Chinese men stand by the kerosene lamp at Occidental and Yesler, more intent on the camera than on the conveyance. The Yesler-Leary Building looms above the rear of the car. Courtesy of Photograph Collection, University of Washington Library

Chinese workers dug a route for the Northern Pacific tracks through the snowfields of Stampede Pass, about 1887. Courtesy of Photograph Collection, University of Washington Library

Colonel Granville O. Haller, a leader of the Home Guard, a local militia group which escorted Chinese residents back to their homes. From History of Seattle *by Frederick Grant; courtesy of Photograph Collection, University of Washington Library*

Judge Thomas Burke was spokesman for opponents of expulsion. From History of Seattle *by Frederick Grant; courtesy of Photograph Collection, University of Washington Library*

Governor Watson C. Squire declared martial law to prevent a trial of Home Guard officers who gave orders to fire on the mob. From Smalley's Magazine, *May 1886; courtesy of Photograph Collection, University of Washington Library*

A Chinese houseboy in Seattle in the 1880s. Courtesy of Photograph Collection, University of Washington Library

Martial law proclamation. Courtesy of Photograph Collection, University of Washington Library

The Chinese were forced to leave their quarters and go to the wharf to board the Queen of the Pacific. *From* West Shore, *1886; courtesy of Photograph Collection, University of Washington Library*

Home Guards fired on anti-Chinese vigilantes in front of the New England Hotel at the corner of Main and Commercial (First Avenue South). The Chinese were inside the square formed by troops under Captain George Kinnear as the rioters tried to break through and get at them. From Harper's Weekly; *courtesy of Photograph Collection, University of Washington Library*

By 1885 loggers had clear-cut the hills behind Seattle, but huge first-growth logs came in by train from the Cascade foothills. Community leaders posed in front of some of the fallen giants near the present site of the Kingdome. Courtesy of Photograph Collection, University of Washington Library

The University of Washington served as a grade school through Seattle's early years, its offerings supplemented by those of various private schools. On January 16, 1869, Seattle voters passed their first millage. A site was purchased and a schoolhouse, two stories tall and forty-eight feet by sixty feet, was erected. The first free common school outside the university opened in the fall of 1870 with Miss L. W. Ordway as the faculty. By 1873 it was overcrowded. Two more schools were built: South School at Main and Sixth, North School at Third and Pine.

In 1874 Professor John N. Hall, who for a time had been president of the university, was selected to head the schools and to reorganize the system. Central School opened at Sixth and

Madison in May 1883, with E. S. Ingraham as principal. It became the first high school in 1886 and burned in 1888. Denny School, built in 1884 at a cost of $35,000, replaced the old North School. Denny was torn down in 1928 during the last regrade.

The Sisters of the Holy Names established the first Catholic school at Second and Seneca in 1880 under the direction of Sister Superior Francis Xavier. Three years later they moved to the academy shown here, at Seventh and Jackson. In 1908 the present Holy Names Academy was built at Twenty-first and East Aloha. From Seattle, published by Charles Kittinger, 1889; courtesy of Photograph Collection, University of Washington Library

Carrie Shumway was one of three
Shumway sisters who taught at Central
School in the 1880s and 1890s. She
also taught at T. T. Minor for a time.
The photo on the stand shows
Snoqualmie Falls, one of the most
popular stock shots of the period.
Courtesy of Seattle Public Schools
Archives

The first Seattle High School graduating class, June 4, 1886. Left to right, seated: Lillie M. White, Belle M. Vrooman, Fannie W. McRae, Emma Ulin, Hadie Gasche. Standing: Axel F. Anderson, Pierre P. Ferry (also shown in the 1889 photo of Seattle's hose laying team), Millie Pickard, Lillie L. Piper, Albert N. Graves, Robert E. Russell, William W. Feas. Courtesy of Seattle Public Library

Females of assorted ages attended the University of Washington. The group represents most of those in attendance in 1884. Courtesy of Photograph Collection, University of Washington Library

Frye's Opera House, completed in 1885 between Madison and Marion on Front Street, dominated the waterfront. John Nester, the architect, patterned the theater after the old Baldwin Theater in San Francisco. The building was four stories high with stores along Front Street and offices on the upper floors.

The main entrance from Marion Street led to a gas-lit, 1,300-seat auditorium decorated with gold and brown curtains, seats upholstered in brown plush with a band of red at the top, draperies in red and gold, a heavy green velvet carpet embellished with red roses, a huge chandelier, and a drop curtain depicting a covered wagon.

The fire of 1889 began at the foot of Madison Street, which is at the extreme left. The houseboat in the right corner was at the foot of Columbia Street. Photograph by A. C. Warner; courtesy of Photograph Collection, University of Washington Library

Western Avenue in 1887, looking north from Pike, a working class district that is now the site of the Pike Place market. Courtesy of Seattle Public Library

The J. J. McGilvra home, known as Laurel Shade, was built beside Lake Washington in what is now the Madison Park neighborhood. Before the extension of Madison Street it was the landing and shipping place for the neighborhood. McGilvra arrived in Seattle in 1864 with an appointment from Abraham Lincoln as U.S. Attorney. There was only one other lawyer in Seattle at the time, and McGilvra prospered, grew with the town, and grew out of it, acquiring this Lake Washington estate. Courtesy of Seattle Public Library

The first cable railway in Seattle was built by J. M. Thompson and Associates and went into operation September 29, 1888. It carried passengers from Second Street out Yesler to Lake Washington and back by way of Jackson Street. It was heavily subsidized by owners of property along the route and for some years was the most profitable streetcar line in the state. The open car in this picture taken at the lake terminal is now in the Smithsonian Institution in Washington, D.C. Its conductor was James Severence. The other men in the picture are not identified. Courtesy of Seattle Public Library

Thompson and Associates continued to build cable lines. They had cars going from King Street to the power house at Denny Way by 1889. A Madison Street line came next and then the James Street cable from the business district to Madrona Park. Here, the tracks pass Fifth and James, now the site of the parking lot across from the county courthouse. Photograph by James Lee; courtesy of Photograph Collection, University of Washington Library

Riders on the James Street line pass the Hotel Kalmar, built at Sixth and James in 1891. Courtesy of Washington State Library

The end of the line—Madrona Park. Courtesy of Photograph Collection, University of Washington Library

Everybody out! Madison Street trolleys backed up behind a derailment. Bystanders risked muddy ankles in the unpaved street. Courtesy of Seattle Public Library

Streetcar lines did more than carry people to playgrounds; they opened outlying areas for settlement. The Fremont district was platted and promoted by L. H. Griffith, who named it for his old hometown, the seat of Dodge County in Nebraska. David Denny was among those who undertook to develop a subsection in May of 1888, but nothing much happened until the Lake Union streetcar line, in which Griffith was deeply involved, started to build a trestle for streetcars across the head of Lake Union. Crews worked from both ends, but Griffith ran out of money before the sections were connected. Others finished the line, and Fremont was annexed to Seattle in 1891. Photograph by D. R. Judkins; photocopy by Mary Randlett, ASMP; courtesy of Photograph Collection, Washington State Library

This engraving of the Fremont district in 1889 contains only a hint of the developments that would transform the north end of Lake Union into a crowded and active waterfront and the hillside into a residential area of modest, comfortable, tree-shaded homes. From Washington Magazine, December 1889; courtesy of Photograph Collection, University of Washington Library

The Latona Bridge, which stood somewhat west of the present University Bridge, provided access to the University District, then called the Brooklyn Community. Portage Bay is to the left, the channel to Lake Union. The picture was taken from the present site of Freeway Hall. Ivar's Salmon House stands in the approximate location of the building on the right. Courtesy of Photograph Collection, University of Washington Library

The Fremont Weir draining Lake Union with the old Stoneway Bridge in the background. Courtesy of Seattle Public Library

Seattle's championship hose-laying team of 1886-1887. Tacomans accused them of ringing in a professional runner who specialized in entering carnival races and running against all comers with a sack of flour on his back. Front row: Charles Woolery, L. P. Ferry. Second row: Max Rostelle, E. Ditweller, E. C. Green, H. K. Struve, F. Fuller, W. H. Clark, Fred Fay. Back row: unknown, George Horton, Bert Huntoon, Fred K. Struve, Pierre P. Ferry, John Jordon, Mott Willard. Courtesy of Photograph Collection, University of Washington Library

A last look eastward up Yesler Way the day before the fire. The Korn Building, which housed Ziba C. Miles's hardware store, is in the left foreground. The Occidental Building is on the corner and the Yesler-Leary Building across Front Street. June had begun like August in 1889. There was no rain. A high pressure area held over the Northwest. Sunny day followed sunny day. Genteel ladies were hard put to avoid a tan. The town was tinder dry.

At two in the afternoon of June 6, an assistant in James McGough's paint shop in the basement of the Pontius Building at First Avenue and Madison Street put a pot of glue on the stove, then threw shavings onto the fire. The glue boiled over, caught fire, and splattered onto a floor littered with wood shavings, some soaked with turpentine.

The Great Seattle Fire had started. Before it burned itself out, fifty-eight blocks—one hundred sixteen acres—were

destroyed. From the foot of University Street east to Front Street, south halfway to Spring Street, east to Second Avenue, along Second to James Street, up James to Third Avenue, along Third to Yesler Way, then to Fourth Street, and from Fourth south to the water's edge—not a single building escaped. No one was killed. Photograph by William Boyd; courtesy of Photograph Collection, University of Washington Library

The same scene on the following day. Oh, light-hearted, industrious Seattle, pushing rapidly to industrial and commercial greatness, with hearts full of cheer and hands so willing to work, to be reduced to ashes in a single afternoon, and to have the sun of prosperity darkened by a cloud of mocking smoke. Seattle Daily Press, *June 7, 1889. Photograph by John P. Soule; courtesy of University of Washington Library*

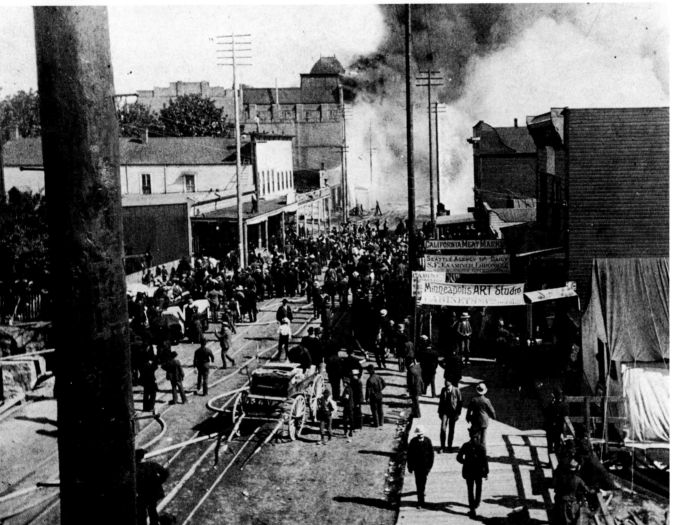

The fire erupted from the Pontius Building on the southwest corner of Front (First) and Madison. This picture was taken looking down Front from Spring Street. The dome of Frye's Opera House can be seen to the left of the smoke. The building on the left side of the street is the M. R. Maddocks drug store. Photograph by Boyd and Braas; courtesy of Seattle Public Library

This etching, based on a photograph, shows the fire as seen from West Seattle. From Harper's Weekly, *June 22, 1889;* *courtesy of Photograph Collection, University of Washington Library*

The Occidental Building, pride of Seattle, after the fire.
 In the heart of the business quarters there was a horrible black smudge, as though a Hand had come down and rubbed the place smooth. Rudyard Kipling in Coast to Coast.
 Photograph by John P. Soule; courtesy of University of Washington Library

Tacomans gathered on the verandah of the Tacoma Hotel to look across Browns Point at the glow in the sky. From Harper's Weekly, *June 22, 1889; courtesy of Photograph Collection, University of Washington Library*

Salvaged possessions guarded by a family dog. From Harper's Weekly, *June 22, 1889; courtesy of Photograph Collection, University of Washington Library*

The First Regiment of the National Guard of Washington was called out to prevent looting. Two guardsmen at the intersection of First and Columbia indicate they mean business. The ruins of the Frye Opera House rise behind the soldiers. Photograph by John P. Soule; courtesy of the Photograph Collection, University of Washington Library

The Dexter Horton bank building at First and Washington was the first all-stone building in Seattle. The bank and the adjoining Harrington & Smith Grocery were the only businesses able to repair their original buildings and go back to work in them. Photograph by John P. Soule; courtesy of Photograph Collection, University of Washington Library

A committee of Tacomans put up a tent, 30-by-120 feet, near the present site of the Post Office on Second Avenue. For a fortnight the Tacomans fed all applicants, the numbers running into the thousands each day. They also provided blankets and sleeping space for those without beds. "Even the Chinese, of whom there were five or six hundred in town, were cared for," says a contemporary account. Courtesy of Seattle Public Library

Seattle guarded its ruins while deciding on reconstruction. The city council took immediate action to turn the fire to Seattle's benefit. Tents could be used as provisional shelter for businesses, but the new downtown was to be of brick, stone, and metal. First Avenue and Occidental would be widened to eighty-four feet, Second Avenue to ninety feet. To facilitate clearing, the city purchased the Yesler Corner, a triangle bordered by Cherry on the west, Yesler Way on the east, and fronting on First Avenue, for $155,000, the highest front-foot price paid in Seattle to that time. Photograph by John P. Soule; courtesy of Photograph Collection, University of Washington Library

Looking north from Marion. Flowers and tents bloom along Second Avenue as the city comes back to life. Photograph by John P. Soule; courtesy of Photograph Collection, University of Washington Library

A canvas roof and starched shirts marked the re-opening of the Stewart & Holmes Drug Company, but not everything could be so quickly restored. A woman wrote Washington Magazine to ask:

Will any of your lady readers tell me how I can clean an old silk dress so as to make it look like new? I am sadly in need of a new dress but since the fire we are obliged to be very economical and having heard that there is a simple way of renovating silk I am in hope that some of your lady readers can give me the recipe, and therefore ask you to publish this inquiry.

A letter in the next issue suggested a compound of "1 cup strong tea and ½ cup unsweetened gin." Photograph by William Boyd; courtesy of Photograph Collection, University of Washington Library

A new courthouse having been built in 1891, King County put the old courthouse at the corner of Third and Jefferson up for auction. The city of Seattle bought it and transformed it into a city hall. Numerous additions across the years earned the structure the nickname of Katzenjammer House. Courtesy of Seattle Public Library

South School's first baseball team in the spring of 1890. With the erection of Rainier, T. T. Minor, Pontius, and Mercer schools in 1890, interschool competition was inaugurated in 1891. Courtesy of Seattle Public Library

The Seattle Female College opened in the Ravenna District in 1891 but burned only two years later, shortly after this picture was taken by a photographer known only as "Professor" Conn. Courtesy of Seattle Public Library

A man and child stand at the curve of the Seattle, Lake Shore, and Eastern in the remote Ravenna area in 1892. The short-lived Seattle Female College can be seen in the background and the two-year-old Seattle Flouring Mill and Granary beside the tracks at the right. Courtesy of Seattle Public Library

Western Union arranged an exhibition of the telephone in Seattle in 1878. A line was run eight miles around the head of the bay from Seattle to West Seattle. Townsfolk lined up to listen as the American Speaking Telephone equipment carried the sounds of voices and the ticking of a watch, but local investors failed to plunge. A franchise was given by the town council to John Kollock in 1881, but the action was followed by silence. Two years later the Pacific Bell Telephone Company won a franchise and began erecting poles and stringing wires. Harriet Hanson Hall was the first operator. Business was conducted from the Western Union office at Second and Cherry Street. By 1889 there were 306 phones in use. On October 16, 1893, the line from Seattle to Portland and Spokane was put in use, with Mayor Ronald of Seattle talking to Mayor Powell of Spokane. The line was 750 miles long and, except for the New York-Chicago telephone line, the longest in the world. These "hello girls" were photographed in the King Street station. Photograph by James P. Lee; courtesy of Seattle Public Library

Jacob Furth, Seattle Electric Company president. From Argus Magazine; courtesy of Photograph Collection, University of Washington Library

The first electric lights to glow in Seattle were on the steamship Willamette, which on the night of July 31, 1881, illuminated four lamps for the elucidation of the assembled populace. The following year two lamps were installed in the Seattle and Walla Walla Railroad Company's sawmill. The town council gave a franchise for the use of streets and alleys for poles, but none were erected. In 1885 the Seattle

Electric Light Company was organized with capital stock of $50,000—but no capital. In 1889 the Seattle Electric Railway and Power Company was formed, and on March 19 the first electric streetcar on the Pacific Coast went into operation. By the 1890s this horse-drawn version of the power company's cherry picker was a familiar sight on Seattle streets. Courtesy of Seattle City Light

The Bailey Gatzert *was launched from John J. Holland's yard on Salmon Bay, November 22, 1890. The 177-foot sternwheeler was tall and elegant, her curved texas deck capped by a sky-scraping pilot house. Built for the Seattle Steam Navigation & Transportation Company, she was purchased in 1891 by the Columbia River & Puget Sound Transportation Company and put on the run between Seattle and Olympia.*

The automobile eventually killed her. When highways replaced the sound as the main line of communication, the Bailey Gatzert *was converted to ferry service between Seattle and Bremerton. She eventually became a floating machine shop on Lake Union. The memory of maritime elegance at its most beautiful lives in this photo showing her against a backdrop of the Olympic Mountains in the early 1890s. Photograph by Frank LaRoche; courtesy of the Photograph Collection, University of Washington Library*

The approach of the Great Northern, which promised Seattle relief from the favoritism that the Northern Pacific showed Tacoma, was celebrated in 1892 with the forecast of direct service east. More than 1,000 miles of track remained to be laid on the trans-continental, but the streetcar, at least, reached Lake Washington. Photograph by D. T. Smith; courtesy of Photograph Collection, University of Washington Library

The forest had been chased north of the city limits by the mid-1890s. From the north slope of Capitol HIll we look westward across Capitol Hill at the stripped expanse of Queen Anne. Photograph by Webster and Stevens; Courtesy of Lou Miller

Chapter 3

THE NOT-SO-GAY NINETIES

1893-1900

The hopes of the early 1890s collapsed with the Panic of 1893. The long depression that followed tested Seattle's resilience. Growth slowed for several years, but in Seattle, unlike Tacoma where there was a severe loss of population, people stayed put. By standing almost still through the worst period, Seattle consolidated its position as dominant city on the sound.

James J. Hill deserved the statues Seattle erected to him in the 1890s. Not only did he bring the Great Northern to town just in time to cushion the shock of the panic, but he also went on to win control of the rival Northern Pacific. No longer did Seattle have to fear that the directors of the Northern Pacific, with heavy personal and corporate investments in the Tacoma Land Company, would favor the southern city over the northern.

Even while the city was growing slowly in population, it was expanding outward. The University of Washington bought its present campus in the Brooklyn district in 1893 and moved onto it in 1895, pulling residential development northward.

Streetcar lines brought the commerce of the new suburbs into the central shopping district.

Still the economy remained pinched. It was claimed that every banker knew the whereabouts of every double eagle (twenty dollar gold-piece) at the end of each day's business. Business forces were routed in the election of 1896 which saw the Populists win the governorship and control of the state legislature and Seattle city council, though the Republicans won the presidency.

Two unrelated events broke the depression and stimulated Seattle's growth: the discovery of gold in the Klondike region of Canada's Yukon Territory and war, the brief, successful war with Spain in 1898 and the long, costly war to suppress the Filipinos who sought independence as a republic rather than association with the United States. The gold rush to the Yukon and later to Nome, as well as the expansion of American trade and naval activity in the Pacific, touched off Seattle's most spectacular period of growth.

The completion of the Great Northern helped cushion Seattle against the Panic of 1893, which devastated its rival, Tacoma, but for the next two years not even the city directory, a wellspring of optimism, claimed growth. When Jacob Coxey of Massilon, Ohio, called for recruits for his Commonwealth Army of Christ—which planned the first protest march on Washington, D.C.—200 men enlisted in the Seattle army the first day, 600 the first week. Here a contingent falls in before moving out for Washington as "a petition with boots on." Photograph by C. L. Andrews; courtesy of Photograph Collection, University of Washington Library

The Commonwealers marched to Puyallup, where they joined a Tacoma contingent, then started across the Cascades, hopping freight cars when they could. Many were arrested after battling sheriffs and deputy marshalls assigned to guard the trains. Five companies of army troops were rushed to Seattle from Vancouver to protect the U.S. District Court when the 'wealers went on trial. Of 157 brought to trial, Judge Cornelius Hanford convicted 121 and gave them sentences ranging from one to sixty days. There was no violence. The troops withdrew. Photograph by C. L. Andrews; courtesy of Photograph Collection, University of Washington Library

The most photographed residence in the 1890s was that of Angeline, daughter of Chief Seattle, friend of the early settlers. It was built from lumber donated by Henry Yesler and was visited by Presidents Hayes and Harrison.

Angeline's friend, Bertha Piper Vernon, wrote in 1903:

And Angeline's shack? Long since it fell
In Way of Progress' path, pell mell;
Thus pass away the things of earth,
The grandest and humblest hearth.

Courtesy of Photograph Collection, University of Washington Library

Although when drunk she sometimes threw clams at the sheriff's house, Princess Angeline was the most popular person in Seattle. When in 1896 she died in the little cabin Henry Yesler had built for her, the townfolk had a coffin made in the form of a canoe, and they turned out for her funeral in such numbers that not all could get into the Church of Our Lady of Good Help. "The well-remembered red bandana covers her head," an obituary noted with patronizing fondness, "and her form is encompassed in a handsome brown shroud. Angeline looks better dead than alive." Courtesy of Gladys Shillestad Kayshor

Caroline "Carrie" McGilvra, the elder daughter of attorney John McGilvra, surprised the town by marrying stumpy (five feet two), erudite Thomas Burke, who had briefly been her father's law partner. She prided herself on her clothes and was often photographed by Edward Curtis, who took this picture. Though often separated in earlier years by her passion for travel, the Burkes spent much time together on foreign trips in their later life. Courtesy of Photograph Collection, University of Washington Library

The southern slope of Capitol Hill was on the outskirts of town in 1895 when this picture was taken from about Broadway and James. The diagonal street across the upper left is Madison Avenue. Courtesy of Seattle Public Library

Before the telescopic camera enabled photographers to magnify the majesty of the mountain on the southeastern horizon, the real estate agents could arrange the same effect. The point of land jutting into Lake Washington from the left, suggesting a small island or the shore of Mercer, is actually part of Seward Park. Courtesy of Photograph Collection, University of Washington Library

WASHINGTON THE EVERGREEN STATE and SEATTLE, ITS METROPOLIS.

MOUNT RAINIER, (14,444 FEET HIGH) FROM SEATTLE.

PUBLISHED BY

FIRST EDITION, 50,000 COPIES.

Crawford & Conover

JANUARY 1890.

REAL ESTATE AND FINANCIAL BROKERS, SEATTLE WASHINGTON.

Everett Smith, later a superior court judge, bought from John Wilson in 1889 a large tract of land which he platted as Brighton Beach addition. Two years later, when the Rainier

Beach streetcar line began operation, the Smiths moved into the Wilson farmhouse. In 1893 Smith employed a carpenter with considerable architectural competence to build a three-

tier treehouse in a giant madrona overlooking Lake Washington.

Standing by the madrona are, left to right: Judge Smith; his father, Eli Stone Smith; his brother, Dr. Clarence A. Smith, co-founder of Northwest Medicine, which he edited for forty-seven years; and Dr. John Trumbull of Valparaiso, Chile, the husband of Flora Smith. The women seated in front of the madrona are Mrs. Clarence Smith and Mrs. Everett Smith, with Harold V. Smith, who is still living in Seattle, at her right side. Mrs. Trumbull, the sister of Everett and Clarence, is in the front row. Courtesy of Harold V. Smith

The lakefront parks were originally owned by the street railway corporations that developed and served them. Working class patrons of Madison Park, Leschi Park, and Madrona Beach rode the cars to the end of the line for a day's amusement, while the more affluent formed summer communities of cottages

and houseboats.

Leschi was the most developed, its attractions including a deer park, a zoological museum, and a seal pen in the lake as well as the inevitable restaurants, boat houses and band stands. Sarah Bernhardt played Camille, in French, in the Leschi

Pavilion in 1895, but most of the entertainment, then as now, lay in strolling, swimming, and admiring Mount Rainier. Courtesy of Photograph Collection, University of Washington Library

A member of Johnson's Canoe Club
heads for the races in the summer of
1897. Argus publisher H. A. Chadwick,
who spent his summers in a luxurious
houseboat on the lake, saluted the
opening of Madison Park with a sniffy
acknowledgment of democracy:

   We have a Coney Island now, a
playground for the Industrials. . . .
The whole is one inharmonious
medley of sounds, and therein lies
the charm of the resort for those who
go there. It is all cosmopolitan to a
degree, mixed, unexclusive—it is of
the people, for the people, by the
people, a democratic arrangement to
always appeal to certain kinds of
Americans.
   Courtesy of Seattle Public Library

There was a fad for canoe jousting, with knights in bathing suits, armed with poles tipped with boxing gloves, vying to dunk each other. Courtesy of Old Seattle Paperworks

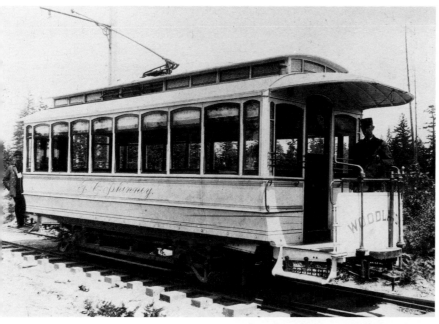

G. C. Phinney owned Woodland as a private park. The grounds were open to the public as long as they obeyed Phinney's rules, which prohibited picking flowers, carrying guns, using "profane, vulgar or improper language" or playing games before noon on Sunday. Dogs were to be shot on sight.

Phinney had a private streetcar that ran to his estate. His name was emblazoned on the side, but the car was usually called the White Elephant. In 1900 the city purchased the 200-acre park, now the site of the Woodland Park Zoo, for $100,000 on what the Argus called "easy terms." Courtesy of Photograph Collection, University of Washington Library

The bicycle as well as the streetcar opened the hinterland to the urban populace. The Good Road Lunchroom was on the old bicycle path that followed what is today Lakeview Boulevard and Interlaken Boulevard. By the end of the century bicyclists could make a fifteen-mile circuit on a view path running over Capitol Hill and out from Lake Union to Lake Washington. George Cotterill, state legislator and mayor-to-be, wrote that the bicycle was "as much a part of the regular transportation life of the city as the streetcar and ordinary steam traffic." He recommended taking Eastern visitors on a bike trip along the path as the way to give them the most favorable impression of Seattle. Courtesy of Seattle Public Library

Bicyclists need rest stops, especially on Queen Anne Hill. These youngsters were photographed around the turn of the century, probably on West Highland. Courtesy of Gerald Johnson

Boys on jungle gym at the public playground, South Fourteenth and Washington, about 1900. Courtesy of Seattle Public Library

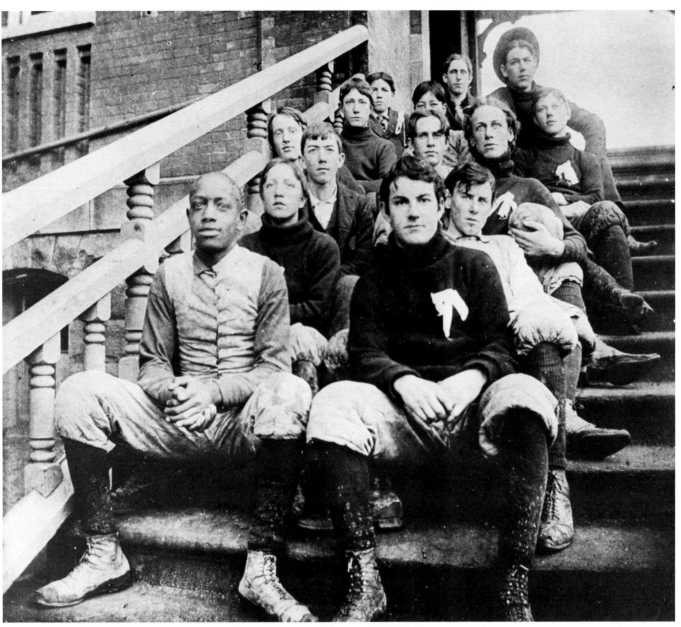

South High School's city championship football team of 1895. Courtesy of Photograph Collection, University of Washington Library

The so-called Twelfth Street Gang of South School was photographed at the turn of the century in front of Kistler's Grocery. Left to right, front row: Harry McGill, Pat McGill, Sam Druxman. Top row: Ollie Helms, Willis Thorpe, "Yorke" Gleason, Bill Hoege, George McCauley, and Joe McGinnis. Courtesy of Seattle Public Library

*Library story hour in a sandbox at a
playfield, about 1900. Courtesy of
Seattle Public Library*

Looking westward down Spokane Street from Beacon Hill at the end of the century. Airport Way would be in the foreground. Courtesy of Photograph Collection, University of Washington Library

Eugene Semple was a failed husband, failed lawyer, failed newspaperman, failed real estate operator. He was no great shakes as a territorial governor either, a position for which a fellow Democrat described him in a letter to the president as "dangerously incompetent, a weak and foolish demagogue . . . a drunken, drooling fool without the capacity for office above that of a poundmaster, [just] another Oregon tramp." Semple died, dead broke, on a $25 a month allowance from his daughters, trying to find backing for a scheme to bypass the Columbia River bar with a canal south of Astoria.

In the 1890s Semple had conceived and got under way a project to connect Puget Sound with Lake Washington by way of a canal through Beacon Hill. The enterprise resulted not in the canal but in the filling in of the industrial marshland below Beacon Hill and, eventually, the creation of Harbor Island, at the time the largest manmade island in the world. From History of Seattle by Frederick Grant; courtesy of Photograph Collection, University of Washington Library

West Seattle's aspirations for a bridge high enough to avoid battering by freighters was noted in 1895 by a cartoonist for Argus. Many collisions and political promises later, a new bridge is under construction.

Salmon Bay Charlie's shack on Shilshole Bay was a Seattle landmark during the 1890s. Charlie, a Suquamish, became Seattle's most popular Indian after the death of Angeline. Courtesy of Ruby Sheurman Wells

Disappointed in 1891 when Congress chose Port Orchard, across the sound, as the site for a naval shipyard, Seattle got its first whiff of benefit from the nascent military-industrial complex when a 640-acre army post, later named Camp Lawton, was established on Magnolia Bluff in 1897.

H. Ambrose Kiehl, a civil engineer employed by the Quartermaster Department, came from Port Townsend to survey the site and supervise construction. Kiehl, who had put himself through Oregon Agricultural College by playing the pipe organ, was a spare man of profuse talents. One was photography, and he managed to take this picture of himself as monarch of all he was surveying from a stump above Shilshore Bay. *Courtesy of Laura Kiehl*

The project engineer for Fort Lawton took his daughter for a ride, circa 1896.

Photo by H. Ambrose Kiehl; courtesy of Laura Kiehl

The engineers were still logging Fort Lawton years later. Logs were bucked into six-foot lengths and stacked around the parade ground for eventual use in the fort's furnaces. Laura and Lorena Kiehl (center and right) pose with a friend from Walla Walla while Mr. Kiehl and another engineer look on. Circa 1910. Photograph by H. Ambrose Kiehl; courtesy of Laura Kiehl

The Stockland sisters—Helena Stockland Semple, Isabella Stockland Buzzard, and Louisa Jean Kiehl—pose in Easter hats and new capes in 1897.

Photograph by H. Ambrose Kiehl; courtesy of Laura Kiehl

A Spanish Jesuit turned Protestant missionary, Dr. Alexander de Soto established the Wayside Mission Hospital in 1899 in the hull of the old sidewheeler Idaho. A donation from Captain Amos O. Benjamin, the hull was drydocked at the foot of Jackson Street. It lacked running water and plumbing, but it was conveniently located for patients from the Skid Road, and operations were performed in it. In 1907 the Oregon Improvement Company took over the site for a railroad extension. The hospital found new quarters at Second and Republican. Two years later, the city took over the care of indigent patients, using facilities in the Public Safety Building. Photo by Anders Wilse; courtesy of Photograph Collection, University of Washington Library

Word of the discovery of gold in the Canadian Yukon reached San Francisco on July 17, 1897. Two days later, 5,000 people were gathered at Schwabacher's Dock at six in the morning for the arrival of the Portland with what was heralded as "a ton of gold." (It proved to be nearly two tons.) Already the Portland was booked full for her return north, and would-be millionaires were bidding for passage on the six other vessels scheduled for Alaska that year. Departures became an important part of life in Seattle. Courtesy of Old Seattle Paperworks

94

So many dogs were sent north that the Argus *described Seattle as "a cat's paradise." Here, a team of harnessed goats passed the Merchant's Cafe at 906 Second Avenue, near Madison. (It was not the Merchants Cafe now in business at 109 Yesler.) Photograph by H. Ambrose Kiehl; courtesy of Laura Kiehl*

Designed to carry 250 passengers at most, the Willamette *had 800 on board when she headed north. Photograph by Anders Wilse; courtesy of Photograph Collection, University of Washington Library*

Seattle's claim to be the focal port for the gold rush was certified by the government with the opening of an assay office at Ninth and James on July 15, 1898. Sourdoughs no longer had to send their dust and nuggets to the mint at San Francisco. During thirty-eight years of operation on James Street, the office handled dust and nuggets worth $414,735,274.66. Some of it rubbed off on the employees; in 1906 the manager of the office pleaded guilty to abstracting dust from some pokes and substituting sand. He served ten years. Photograph by Asahel Curtis; courtesy of Photograph Collection, University of Washington Library

There was little deck space left on most gold rush ships. Photograph by H. Ambrose Kiehl; courtesy of Laura Kiehl

Not everybody struck it rich. For instance, the mayor of Seattle, W. D. Wood, was in San Francisco when the Excelsior *arrived with the first reports of Klondike gold. He bought the handsome steamship* Humboldt *and chartered her to prospectors for the run to Saint Michael at the mouth of the Yukon, but the party suffered nearly a year's delay in reaching the goldfields. A huge crowd of wasp-waisted women and straw-hatted men greeted the* Humboldt *when she returned from the north and docked in Seattle, but her owner had only experience to show for the venture. Photograph by Asahel Curtis; courtesy of Photograph Collection, University of Washington Library*

U.S.A.T. ROSECRANS AND LAWTON FROM UNIVERSITY ST. INCLINE

Congress declared war on Spain on April 11, 1898. An armistice was arranged on August 12, but a day later American forces in the Philippines, not having heard the news, stormed Manila. In this photograph by Theodore Peiser, the army transports Rosecrans *and* Lawton *are tied up at the foot of University Street awaiting the loading of troops in the fall of 1898. Courtesy of Photograph Collection, University of Washington Library*

The first contingent of Washington volunteers returned aboard the transport Queen *on November 6, 1899, to be greeted by pennant-decked yachts, tugs, and steamers. Photograph by Anders Wilse; courtesy of Photograph Collection, University of Washington Library*

The Pioneer Square totem was stolen from the Tlingit village of Tongass in 1899 by a group of Seattle businessmen on a good will cruise to Alaska. The culprits were later fined, but Seattle kept the totem and in October erected it in the square. The original was damaged by fire in 1938. When inspected, it was found to be ruined by dry rot. A copy was carved in Saxman, near Ketchikan, and re-dedicated in 1940.

The totem is unusual in that it is dedicated to a woman, Chief-of-All-Women, who drowned in the Nass River while going to visit her sister.

The figures from the top down represent Raven holding a crescent moon in his beak; a woman with a frog child; the woman's frog husband; Mink; Raven; Whale with Seal in his mouth; and at the bottom, the Grandfather of Raven. From an 1899 postcard; courtesy of Photograph Collection, University of Washington Library

Volunteers Return
Seattle Nov 6th 99.

The American military presence in the Far East did not end with the Spanish-American War. A detachment of Troop C of the 9th Cavalry stood in front of its tents at Camp Lawton on August 10, 1900, shortly before embarking for China to join an international force of British, French, Russian, German, and Japanese troops assembled to suppress the Boxer uprising against foreign and Christian influence. Photograph by Theodore Peiser; courtesy of Photograph Collection, University of Washington Library

The traffic cop was still king of the street in the early 1900s. This one reflectively adjusts his helmet and studies the cobbles on Westlake. The Westlake Mall monorail station now stands below the hanging sign which reads Outbound Cars Stop On This Crossing Only. Courtesy of Seattle Public Library

Chapter

SEATTLE AS METROPOLIS

1900-1910

By 1900 Seattle stood unchallenged as the metropolis of Puget Sound and Washington State, its only rival in the region, Portland.

The sound had been the highway for the pioneers just as it was for the Indians, but patterns of transportation were changing. Although larger and faster steamships provided swift and frequent service between the ports, it was becoming increasingly easy to get about on land. Trunk railroads sprouted feeder lines. Streetcars drew shoppers and workers from developing suburbs, and annexations followed. Interurbans sped down the north-south valleys, hinting at the Pugetopolis to come. The automobile made its appearance.

Life for the middle class was comfortable. The city offered many pleasures, the countryside even more. It was wonderful to be young and affluent in a confident city. Progress and growth were the watchwords. As gold continued to flow in from the north, silk and tea from the Orient, and population from everywhere, Seattle expanded vertically with buildings of eight, ten, and twelve stories as well as horizontally along the streetcar lines of the developers and the boulevards suggested by the Olmsted Brothers, landscape architects. But the hills of home were considered a liability.

For better and for worse, there was in Seattle a man obsessed with the idea of removing hills. As some feel a call to the ministry, Reginald H. Thomson felt a call to level land. From the day of his arrival in 1881 (the day of the memorial service for President Garfield), he dreamed of flattening Denny Hill, reducing north-south grades from their maximum of twenty percent to no more than three percent, and carrying traffic through the business district on streets ninety feet wide.

"That Man Thomson," as his opponents called him, did not quite turn Seattle into Kansas City, but in the first phase of the Denny Hill regrade he directed the movement of 5 million cubic yards of dirt from the slopes west of Fifth Avenue onto low spots throughout the downtown area and onto the tideflats below the First Avenue bluff. In the late

The Renton Express headed south along Lake Washington through a stand of young alders. The twelve-mile line was in operation by 1900. Courtesy of Frank McClelland

1920s the uphill area between Fifth Avenue and Ninth was sluiced away according to the Thomson plan. Thomson created the topography that those who came to Seattle in the past fifty years think of as nature's work.

As Seattle grew conscious of its success, it decided to throw a party in honor of itself. A few old-timers playing dominoes in the Alaska Club after lunch one afternoon in 1905 started discussing ways the city might celebrate in 1907 the tenth anniversary of the discovery of gold on the Klondike. Out of the bull session came the Alaska-Yukon-Pacific (AYP) Exposition.

The AYP opened two years after the target date but nonetheless was a phenomenal success. More than 3,740,000 visitors went through the gates, paying $1,095,366 in admission fees. The Expo people proved expert in raising outside funds, especially government funds. When the books were closed, AYP had an astonishing $785,211.10 left over.

Even better, the University of Washington received as AYP heritage a campus landscaped to a design by the Olmsted Brothers and buildings that were to serve generations of students. Of the $1,000,000 appropriated by the state legislature for the exposition, $600,000 went for three permanent buildings, including the awkward but beloved Meany Hall and Bagley Hall. Many structures designated temporary remained in use fifty years later.

Half a century after the AYP, City Councilman Al Rochester recalled the story of the exposition and the wonder of being young in Seattle in the early years of the twentieth century:

It wasn't just the Pay Streak with its games, or the *Monitor* fighting the *Merrimac*, or the Igorrote village where the girls' costumes satisfied a lot of boyish curiosity. It was the whole thing—the concerts at the Music Pavilion, the Eskimo Village, the Cascades—a pond that was a waterfall, the Forestry Building where every log weighed twenty-five tons and contained enough board feet to build five houses. It was the bagpipers, and the coming of the president, and the speech by William Jennings Bryan where his admirers stormed the platform, crazy as bobby soxers, and broke up the furniture for souvenirs and ripped the silver buttons off the Great Commoner's Prince Albert coat, and I was there on the platform, clutching his coattails.

There were warships in Elliott Bay—Japanese as well as American—and at night their searchlights would chase each other across the sky. The first cross-country auto race, New York to Seattle, finished on the fairgrounds. A Ford won, in twenty three days, and Henry Ford was there to welcome the winner, though I don't remember that he was famous then. Special trains came up from California, twenty coaches long, with smoking permitted on every coach, and the mail and telegrams delivered at each stop. People on the streets spoke languages you couldn't understand; couldn't even guess what they were.

Oh, the wonder of it! And it was all happening right here in Seattle. (Albert Rochester, 1962).

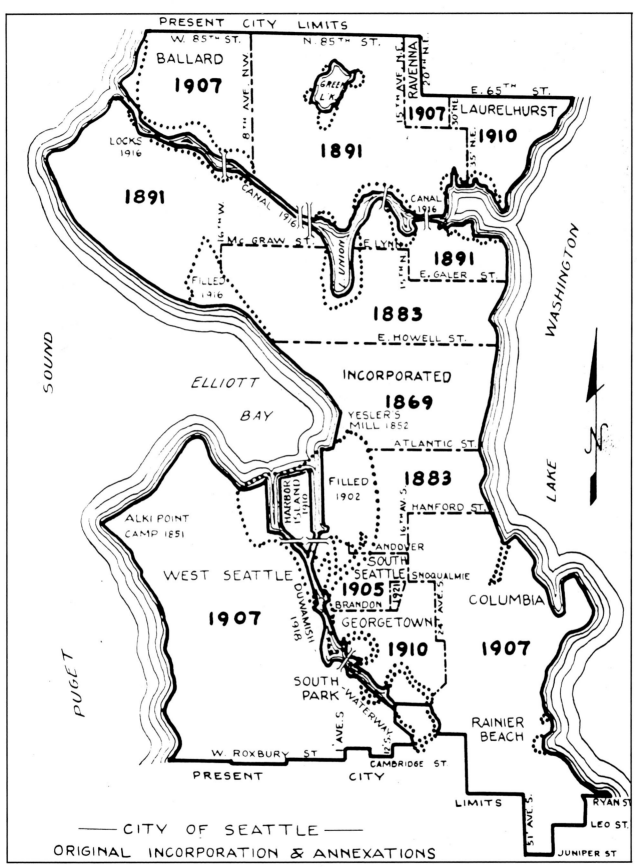

PRESENT CITY LIMITS

W. 85TH ST.   N. 85TH ST.

BALLARD
1907

RAVENNA
1907

LAURELHURST
1910

E. 65TH ST.

GREEN LK.

1891

LOCKS 1916

CANAL 1916

CANAL 1916

1891

McGRAW ST.

FILLED 1916

UNION

E. LYN

1891

E. GALER ST.

1883

E. HOWELL ST.

SOUND

ELLIOTT BAY

INCORPORATED
1869

YESLER'S MILL 1852

WASHINGTON

LAKE

ATLANTIC ST.

FILLED 1902

1883

HANFORD ST.

HARBOR ISLAND 1910

ALKI POINT CAMP 1851

ANDOVER

SOUTH SEATTLE

SNOQUALMIE

COLUMBIA

1907

WEST SEATTLE

1907

DUWAMISH 1918

BRANDON

1905

GEORGETOWN

1910

PUGET

SOUTH PARK

WATERWAY

RAINIER BEACH

W. ROXBURY ST.

CAMBRIDGE ST.

PRESENT   CITY   LIMITS

RYAN ST.

LEO ST.

JUNIPER ST.

— CITY OF SEATTLE —
ORIGINAL INCORPORATION & ANNEXATIONS

Annexations followed the extension of streetcar lines and boulevards. This map, prepared by the Seattle City Engineer in 1938, shows the spread of the city from the time of first settlement through the annexations of 1910. Courtesy of Photograph Collection, University of Washington Library

105

Photos in an old family album now in the possession of Gerald Johnson, a Seattle antique dealer, show the pleasures of Seattle living for an upper middle class family. Baron Duffy owned the Rainier Bakery on First Avenue and lived in a large, comfortable frame house on West Highland atop Queen Anne Hill.

Here, the family has gathered for a picnic at the edge of town. Courtesy of Gerald Johnson

Edward Duffy, the elder son, shown here cleaning his gun, borrowed the company delivery wagon for a shooting expedition with friends. Courtesy of Gerald Johnson

Gilbert Duffy, the younger son, prepares for tea in the side yard. Courtesy of Gerald Johnson

The Duffy women and friends sew in the backyard. Courtesy of Gerald Johnson

A picture of the U.S.S. Nebraska, *a Seattle favorite, hangs in the corner of the second floor sitting room. Courtesy of Gerald Johnson*

Ned Duffy was an athlete, a Sigma Nu, and something of a ladies' man. He won letters in baseball, football, and track at the University of Washington and played but did not letter in basketball. Here we see him before the game with Washington Agricultural College in 1901. Courtesy of Gerald Johnson

This locker room shot is called "watching basketball" in the family album. That seems unlikely. Courtesy of Gerald Johnson

A Sigma Nu picnic in 1902, location unknown. Courtesy of Gerald Johnson

Ed Duffy poses with a kissin' cousin.
Courtesy of Gerald Johnson

It was Gilbert who won the girl across Highland Street—Florence Blethen, daughter of the publisher of the Seattle Times. *Courtesy of Gerald Johnson*

In 1903 the Olmsted Brothers, sons of landscape artist Frederick Law Olmsted, presented the Seattle Park Board with the design for a twenty-mile parkway to connect most of the city's existing and proposed parks and greenbelts. Not all of the Olmsted proposals were carried out, but many portions were, including the lovely Lake Washington Boulevard, seen in this 1912 photo. Photograph by Webster and Stevens; courtesy of Lou Miller

The coming of automobiles eventually forced the owners of the passenger steamer Chippewa *to cut a garage door in her bow and turn her into a ferry, but there was no hint of such a fate at the passenger terminal when this picture was taken in 1908. Courtesy of Old Seattle Paperworks*

When Robert Moran came to Seattle in 1875, he couldn't find work as a machinist so he shipped out on a steamboat. By 1882 he had saved $1,500 with which he set up a small machine shop beside Yesler wharf. Moran prospered and was serving as mayor when the shop was destroyed in the fire of 1889. Instead of rebuilding the machine shop, he started a small shipyard. During the gold rush it turned out a fleet of twelve identical riverboats for service on the Yukon. Photograph by H. Ambrose Kiehl; courtesy of Laura Kiehl

In 1902 Moran won the contract to build a battleship, the U.S.S. Nebraska. Cartoon from Argus Magazine, *1903; courtesy of Photograph Collection, University of Washington Library*

The keel of the Nebraska *was laid
July 4, 1902. The hull hit the water
October 7, 1904. Naval architecture
was changing so rapidly that the
finished battlewagon bore little resemblance to the original plans. Photograph
by Asahel Curtis; courtesy of Photograph Collection, University of
Washington Library*

*The bow-wave from the U.S.S.
Nebraska nearly swamped the tugboat
from which Asahel Curtis took this
picture of the ship's official naval test
cruise. The Nebraska reached a peak
speed of slightly more than 19½ knots
on the run. Moran had protested in
vain against Navy Board requirements
that the anchor be dropped while the
ship was moving at full speed. When the
hook was let go, the chain snapped and
the anchor was lost. Moran used the
links that were left as a fence for his
mansion at Rosario on San Juan
Island, where he retired in 1906 after
being told he was dying. He lived there
for forty years. Photograph by Asahel
Curtis; courtesy of Seattle Public
Library*

The narrow strip between Lake Union and Lake Washington was known as the Portage. It had been the scene of an early canal-digging effort by Harvey L. Pike, who in 1860 had started breaking ground with a pick but soon gave up. Later, a narrow ditch was dug so logs from the shores of Lake Washington could be snaked through as well as barges bearing coal brought down from the mines at Newcastle and Coal Creek. Completion of the railroad to the mines ended barge service, but when this picture was taken from the south slope of Capitol Hill, a raft of logs from the larger lake floated in Portage Bay. In the background lies Laurelhurst, which had been clear-cut to make space for the proposed sawmill town of Yesler. *Courtesy of Photograph Collection, University of Washington Library*

The Seattle Golf Club near today's Laurelhurst. Asahel Curtis took this picture from the fourth tee looking toward the club house on April 19, 1902. *Courtesy of Photograph Collection, University of Washington Library*

118

Electric railway service to West Seattle was established after the district's annexation in 1907. One of the beneficiaries of the line was Luna Amusement Park on Duwamish Head, which reached its height of popularity in the next five years. The park burned in 1931. Courtesy of Washington State Library

Among the attractions at Luna Park were bathing beauties. Max Loudon, an early newsreel photographer, had an eye for them. Photograph by Max Loudon; courtesy of Grace Loudon McAdam

Woodland Park 1903

Three school children admired the view
in Woodland Park during the winter
of 1903. Photograph by "Professor"
Conn; courtesy of Photograph Collection,
University of Washington Library

A turn-of-the-century portrait of Alice
Warner, taken at Green Lake by her
father, the commercial photographer
A. C. Warner. Warner improved on the
natural setting by adding painted
flowers and foliage to the background.
Mrs. Alice Warner Laribee now lives in
Olympia. Courtesy of Photograph
Collection, University of Washington
Library

*The Greenlake Confectionery, circa
1909, sold cigars as well as candy.
Courtesy of Old Seattle Paperworks*

*A Norwegian immigrant and a quartet
of Holsteins in the Ross section of
Fremont before 1910. Courtesy of Chris
Carlsen and the* Fremont Forum

Seattle weather is conducive to reading. Catherine Maynard opened a room in her house as a free reading room after Doc Maynard's death in 1873. The first Library Association was organized in 1868 with James McNaught as president and Mrs. Yesler as librarian. After nine years the association's books were moved into the YMCA.

A public library was established in 1888 by the women of Seattle on a site donated by Yesler. The books were moved to the Occidental Hotel in 1891, then to the Collins Building in 1894, the Rialto Building at Second and Madison in 1895, and the Yesler Mansion at Third and Yesler in 1899.

On New Year's Day, 1901, the library burned. Only 2,000 of the books in the building were saved, but another 5,000 that were on loan were returned. After operating for a month out of the Yesler barn, the library moved into the former University of Washington building, where it remained until the Carnegie Library, shown here, opened December 19, 1906 at Fourth and Madison, the site of the present main library. Courtesy of Seattle Public Library

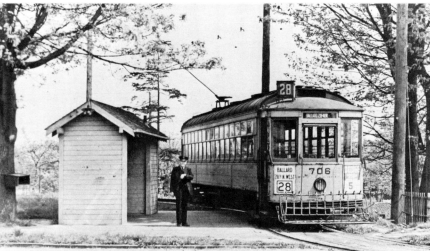

Old 28 won't start up twenty-eighth Northwest until the conductor's watch says the time is right. Courtesy of Frank McClelland

Streetcar strikes were frequent. Motormen worked long hours, were required to stand throughout their shift, and could be fired for leaning against the front of the car. On March 27, 1903, streetcar workers blocked the tracks with horse and wagon and removed a strikebreaker from the car. Photograph by Asahel Curtis; courtesy of Photograph Collection, University of Washington Library

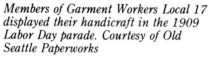

Members of Garment Workers Local 17
displayed their handicraft in the 1909
Labor Day parade. Courtesy of Old
Seattle Paperworks

City Councilman Frank Muldoon
championed Thomson's proposals for the
leveling of Denny Hill and Jackson
Street. From Argus Magazine; courtesy
of Photograph Collection, University of
Washington Library

A regiment of surveyors under the command of City Engineer Thomson prepares to deploy for battle against Seattle's tilted topography. Courtesy of Old Seattle Paperworks

A biographer of Doc Maynard claims "he invented Seattle." A biographer of Arthur Denny claims that dour personage created the framework for the city's growth. A biographer of Judge Burke, quoting from an obituary, says "he built Seattle."

Reginald Thomson flattened Seattle. From That Man Thomson; courtesy of University of Washington Press

The Denny Hill neighborhood, with the handsome Washington Hotel on the bluff overlooking the bay, and the synagogue in center foreground, *disappeared in the decade after Arthur C. Warner took this photo from Ninth and Madison. Smoke hazes Magnolia Hill, which was being clear-cut and* *slash-burned. Courtesy of Photograph Collection, University of Washington Library*

The Washington Hotel was long under construction but short-lived. Arthur Denny had thought of its site as suitable for the state capital and reserved two blocks at the crest of Denny Hill for that purpose. When he regretfully conceded that Seattle wouldn't become the capital, Denny offered the area free to anyone who would build a first class hotel. A public subscription drive in 1891 raised $200,000, and work was well under way when the Panic of '93 brought construction to a halt. In 1900 the unfinished building was claimed by the Denny estate and a Portland bank, which spent another quarter million on its completion. For two years it stood empty; then a flamboyant developer, James A. Moore, bought hotel and site for $250,000, spent another $150,000 on refurbishing, plumbing, and furniture for the 250 rooms, and opened for business in May of 1903, with President Theodore Roosevelt as the first guest to be registered. Photograph by Webster and Stevens; courtesy of Lou Miller

The steam engine and the horse-drawn cart combined to remove much of the glacial till that descended on the Seattle area as the last continental ice-sheet retreated 14,000 or so years ago. The camera here is looking north across Third Avenue at its intersection with University. The Plymouth Congregational Church is on the left. Courtesy of Seattle Public Library

Buildings to be preserved were set on beams supported by a framework of ties. Some structures were simply lowered to the new surface created below. Others were moved to new locations a mile or more away. Many were burned or dismantled. The photographer was standing at Fourth Avenue, looking north from Pine Street. Courtesy of Seattle Engineering Department

From R. L. Polk, Seattle City Directory, 1912; courtesy of Photograph Collection, University of Washington Library

Water pumped under high pressure washed cuts thirty or forty feet deep. Residences were presented with a gulch for a neighbor. Courtesy of Seattle Public Library

In 1905 the Washington Hotel stood on the brink of destruction. Many joined James Moore in resisting its demolition, but the chorus was louder on the theme that "the commercial needs of Seattle demand level streets and skyscrapers." Convinced that the growth of the city northward would raise the value of his property, Moore consented to have the building torn down and claimed no damages from the city.

Judge Thomas Burke, no foe of progress, was among those who mourned its loss:

"Denny Hill has always been one of the most prominent and beautiful eminences of the city," he told the Post-Intelligencer, "and it is doubtful if there is any city the size of Seattle that has a hotel so accessible and commanding so beautiful a view. In this view, destruction of the Washington Hotel will be irreparable as there is no other point in the city from which the same advantages could be obtained. From a commercial point of view and certainly from an aesthetic one it would have been better to have saved Denny Hill by carrying Third Avenue under it, thus obtaining the desired result while preserving the natural beauty that means so much to any city. . . . I do not believe there will ever be a hotel built in the country that will equal it from the standpoint of natural location and beauty."

The Washington as seen looking north across the intersection of Second and Pine. Photograph by Webster and Stevens; courtesy of Photograph Collection; University of Washington Library

A closing week menu for "the scenic hotel of the world." Courtesy of Photograph Collection, University of Washington Library

130

Looking north up Fourth Avenue from slightly south of Stewart in 1910. Photograph by James P. Lee; courtesy of Photograph Collection, University of Washington Library

Regrade routes followed the pattern of city streets. Spikes were left, temporarily, in the middle of blocks. This picture was taken in 1910 from a spot near the intersection of Fourth Avenue and Stewart Street. Postcard photograph by O. T. Frasch; courtesy of Photograph Collection, University of Washington Library

Denny School, now minus a wing, keeps the flag flying as the engineers atop a knoll look out from the east bank of Fifth Avenue from about Blanchard as the first phase of the regrade comes to a close in 1911. Courtesy of Photograph Collection, University of Washington Library

Seattle continued to boom throughout the regrade, hardly feeling the national recession of 1907. Businesses big and small flourished downtown. Ye Olde Curiosity Shop, which opened in 1899 at the Colman Dock, was a curiosity itself. Its wares included the jaw bones of a whale, a carved elephant one thirty-second of an inch tall, a Yellow Sea crab measuring thirteen feet from claw to claw, the Lord's Prayer on the head of a pin, a sixty-seven-pound snail, and an 800-year-old Chinese dog of blue vitreous porcelain.

J. E. Standley, the proprietor, is shown leaning against the totem on the right. He enjoyed trying to explain to small boys what made a duck-billed platypus unusual. Now at 601 Alaskan Way, the shop remains one of the waterfront's most popular attractions. Photograph by Asahel Curtis; courtesy of Photograph Collection, University of Washington Library

The southwest corner of First and Yesler, around 1910. The Pioneer Dentist site at 95 Yesler is once again a dentist's office. The Dinham-Strehlau Shoe Company (We Shoe Children with the Greatest Care) has been replaced by an Italian ice cream parlor. Photograph by C. F. Todd; courtesy Photograph Collection, University of Washington Library

This landscape of the moon picture was taken from a few feet north of Bell Street and a few feet west of Fourth Avenue in 1910. The view is to the south. Photograph by Asahel Curtis; courtesy of Photograph Collection, University of Washington Library

The Pike Place Public Market, one of Seattle's most beloved institutions, was organized in 1907 to allow small truck farmers to sell their goods directly to the public. Originally housed in a single building at First Avenue and Pike, the market has expanded to cover more than three blocks. Besides the stalls for vegetables, meats, and seafoods, there are now restaurants, a theater, stands for handicrafts, and a fascinating array of pedestrians. Courtesy of Seattle Public Library

Christina Christopher was the owner of
this woman-operated barber shop at
1106½ First Avenue, photographed
about 1904. "Such ladies' barber shops
were fairly common at this time,"
according to the Pacific Northwest
Labor History Association. "They were
respectable businesses where the ladies
gave excellent shaves and haircuts,
nothing more and nothing less."
Photograph by Webster and Stevens;
courtesy of the Pacific Northwest Labor
History Association and the Photograph
Collection, University of Washington
Library

The 1907 vendors were exposed to the
weather, but the customers had a
canopy. Courtesy of Washington State
Library

The newlywed A. R. Nelsons pose with friends in front of their Pike Place Market stall. A sampling of signs: Cheese It. I'm married now, don't flirt with me; Extra fine pickled pigs feet in jelly, 20 cents each; and You can have my stall but not my wife. Courtesy of Washington State Library

Kwong Wa Chong Company, an import store at 114 Second Avenue South, taken in 1909. Courtesy of Photograph Collection, University of Washington Library

The Rainier Valley Market in Columbia City. Owner Charlie Nelson is at left. Courtesy of Butch Nelson

Guise Brothers Grocery, on Twentieth near Madison, about 1910. Courtesy of John and Lael Hanawalt, Old Seattle Paperworks

S. H. Hall Grocers, down the street from Guise Brothers at 1928 Madison, made deliveries. Photograph, 1906, courtesy of John and Lael Hanawalt, Old Seattle Paperworks

The Montera Pharmacy in Rainier Beach, 1909. The man with the mustache, second from right, is Dr. Joseph Hutchinson, father of Fred and Dr. Bill Hutchinson. Courtesy of Seattle Public Library

The Alaska-Yukon-Pacific exposition of 1909 was held on the campus of the University of Washington. More than $380,000 was spent on grading and landscaping alone. (Letters to the student paper complained that the native beauty of the site was being destroyed.) Many of the temporary buildings were pressed into service by the school.

    The Washington State Building became the University Library, improved by the addition of a fireproof stack area big enough to house 100,000 volumes. The California Building served first as a museum, later as the student Commons. The university president lived on the upper floors of the New York Building, while the lower floor was used for student functions. The Oregon Building was assigned to the Law School, and the Educational Building housed the departments of education and journalism. Geyser Fountain, seen in the center of this picture taken from a captive balloon, became today's Frosh Pond. Photograph by F. H. Nowell, official AYP photographer; courtesy of Photograph Collection, University of Washington Library

D. C. Hamson, writing in the Seattle Star, was more impressed by the performance of the second-place car, a sedan called the Shamut and described as "a comfortable, roomy touring car weighing 4,000 pounds," than with that of the stripped down, prize-winning Ford. He asked:

Of what use is the rushing, tearing, bumping little motorcycle to the average man, even if it can beat anything in sight? Who wants to go tearing around the countryside alone? What does the average auto buyer want? Surely a car that can carry himself and his family or his friends with him. A big car that is comfortable and roomy. A car that can carry some impedimenta. A car that can endure and that is reliable, and that can speed some, too, if speed is wanted in a pinch. Courtesy of Photograph Collection, University of Washington Library

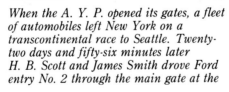

When the A. Y. P. opened its gates, a fleet of automobiles left New York on a transcontinental race to Seattle. Twenty-two days and fifty-six minutes later H. B. Scott and James Smith drove Ford entry No. 2 through the main gate at the

Exposition. Henry Ford presented the victors with $2,000 and a trophy put up by M. Robert Guggenheim. Courtesy of Photograph Collection, University of Washington Library

Edmond S. Meany, professor of forestry at the University of Washington and a Republican state legislator in 1893, chaired the House committee that selected the site for the new University of Washington campus. Later, as a member of the AYP committee, he carried the fight to stage the exposition on the campus so that it would leave more than pleasant memories. Argus Magazine *cartoon; courtesy of Photograph Collection, University of Washington Library*

141

Most distinguished of the visitors to the exposition was the newly inaugurated president of the United States, William Howard Taft, shown here putting his 300 pounds into a six-foot putt at the Seattle Golf Club. Taft won an exhibition match, 2 and 1. Courtesy of Photograph Collection, University of Washington Library

Any major exposition demands a dispute over nudity. How else is attention to be drawn to other things being exposed? The AYP did not violate convention. It did, however, take a unique approach. The fuss focussed on the G-strings worn by the men of an Igorrote village that had been imported from the Philippines to demonstrate that Seattle was interested in the entire Pacific Rim, not just the Yukon and Alaska.

People proclaiming themselves the voice of morality denounced the jock-straps worn by the male Igorrotes as ill-fitting offenses against the purity of females visiting the exposition in innocent belief that they would be exposed to nothing more than culture. A top-hatted committee of personages of ponderous and certifiable probity was created to pass moral judgment on Igorrote attire. Included in its membership were the Reverend Mark Matthews (left), Governor Marion E. Hay, exposition president J. E. Chilberg, and (foreground) Judge Thomas E. Burke. With the Reverend Mr. Matthews casting the deciding vote, the committee decreed the Igorrote breachclouts to be decent. Photograph by Frank Nowell; courtesy of Photograph Collection, University of Washington Library

142

The Pay Streak, offering sedate gambling and decorous dancing girls, was always jammed, though the state legislature would not bend the law to allow liquor to be served on the university grounds.

The oriental dancers were allegedly from Greece, Turkey, Algiers, and Egypt. Princess Zamara, seated on the right, was the sex sensation of the AYP. She fondled live snakes during her love dream dance. But Zamara and her sister exotics drew paid admissions of $43,587 as compared to $139,596 for a concession which featured a rematch of the battle between the Monitor and the Merrimac. Photograph by Frank Nowell; courtesy of Photograph Collection, University of Washington Library

Statuary at the AYP combined the classic with the bizarre. Here a heroic goddess dangles the wires of communication while stroking a salmon. Photograph by Will Hudson; courtesy of Jean Hudson Lunzer

The buoyancy of the AYP came from the belief that development equated with progress. Nowhere was the idea more happily manifest than in the Cascades, the man-made waterfall which rose in front of the main Exposition Building and drained into today's Frosh Pond. Photograph by Dobbs; courtesy of Old Seattle Paperworks

Established in 1887 and given its current name to honor veterans of the Spanish-American War, Volunteer Park illustrates some of the landscaping principles of the Olmsted brothers, whose ambitious plans for Seattle's parks were partially implemented. Native undergrowth was removed and replaced with exotic shrubs as they suggested. The Olmsteds also disliked Douglas firs, claiming that they were "mean and crowded at close quarters" and unable to survive pollution from factory smoke. "Fir trees, in fact all conifers, and evergreens would better be removed at once," they opined. Nevertheless, firs remain in this 1910 photo, and remain still.

Chapter **5**

THE PROGRESSIVE YEARS:

REFORM AND STRIFE

1910-1920

Politics in Seattle had revolved around control of the state legislature by the railroads and control of city hall by the vice interests. Attempts to change the situation resulted in an odd alliance of urban populists, prohibitionists, woman suffragists and progressive Republicans. Though they lost most of the battles in the early stages, many of their campaigns were won in the second decade of the century.

"Honest Tom" Humes, a mayor subject to financial persuasion, had served three consecutive terms starting in 1906 although under steady attack from foes as various as the Reverend Mark Matthews, a Presbyterian divine who prowled the red light district in broad-brimmed hat and deaconly black suit, sniffing brimstone, and city councilman Hiram C. Gill, a scrawny lawyer who affected a corncob pipe and baggy suits.

Hi Gill was elected mayor in 1910 on his promise to run an open town but to confine sin to the Skid Road. He kept the first half of his promise. When Gill approved the leasing of a city street on Beacon Hill to some business friends so they could erect the world's largest brothel—500 rooms!—Seattle's first recall campaign was launched.

The election was lively. Women, who had just regained the ballot in Washington, organized for purity under the slogan: "Ladies: Get out and Hustle." Gill acknowledged that his opponent in the recall election had not been in politics long enough to have enemies, but added, "His friends can't stand him." George Dilling won anyway.

Defeated in 1912 when he ran again as an apologist for regulated vice, Gill campaigned in 1914 as a man experienced enough to know how to run a closed town. Elected, he spent two years sending the vice squad out to raid suspected purveyors of illegal alcohol. Re-elected in 1916, this time with the enthusiastic support of the Reverend Mr. Matthews, he opened the town wide, only to be destroyed politically when the U.S. military authorities undercut his base of support by placing Seattle off limits.

The creation of the Port of Seattle in 1911 was part of the same reformist drive that ejected Hi Gill from office earlier that year.

Some of the port's promoters equated municipal ownerships of docks and wharves with right living, just as they hoped that elimination of private franchises for public services like streetcars and electricity would lessen opportunities for graft. The Reverend J. M. Wilson delivered a sermon in 1906 on "The Moral Value of the Municipal Ownership of Street Railways." On the University of Washington campus, J. Allen Smith, an iconoclastic professor of political science, lectured on "The Trust Problem" and joined campaigns for public ownership. In the business community there was worry about a Tacoma revival and concern that the railroads and the private wharf owners were crippling growth of waterborne commerce.

On September 5, 1911, King County voters by a margin of more than 3 to 1 voted to create an independent municipal corporation, the first of its

Looking north on Fourteenth Street toward the water tower in Volunteer Park about 1910. A private gate at Fourteenth and Roy shielded these dwellers on "Millionaire's Row"— Cobbs, Whites, Stuarts, Skinners, and others—from intrusion until their shrubbery grew up to give them privacy. Courtesy of Photograph Collection, University of Washington Library

kind in the country, to run the port. The port had the power to level taxes and issue bonds. Three commissioners were elected to serve without pay. They were: General Hiram M. Chittenden, who had come to Seattle to supervise construction of the Salmon Bay locks which bear his name; C. E. Remsberg; and Robert Bridges, an unapologetic socialist. Railroad interests and private wharf owners fought back, and port projects were delayed for years by court battles. It was not until the mid-1920s that animosity died down enough to allow the cooperation with private industry that now is a major characteristic of Port of Seattle operations.

Demands for change produced social strain, especially demands by labor for better pay and working conditions. A turn-down in the national economy in the early years of the decade, the failure of the completion of the Panama Canal in 1914 to trigger a new boom, the growth of the radical Industrial Workers of the World in the lumber camps and wheat fields, and the Communist takeover in Russia during World War I led many citizens to equate union demands with a call for revolution. Though the Seattle general strike in 1919 demonstrated the power of labor to shut down the town, and though it ended without violence, it marked the disintegration of the old progressive alliance and the end of a period of social reform.

By the early 1900s, Seattle was genteel enough to support drug and alcohol treatment centers which stressed confidentiality and beautiful views. The Keeley Institute, still standing at 3431-3433 Meridian Avenue in Wallingford, advertised in the 1909 Polk Directory *that it "overlooks Lake Union and gives a scenic view of Seattle, with the Cascade Mountains showing in the distance." It promised cures for liquor, drug, and tobacco addictions as well as nervous exhaustion.*

An even more elaborate retreat for drug addicts was established around the same time in a former Mercer Island resort hotel built by C. C. Calkins. A financial failure as a hotel after Calkins spent a reported $50,000 on the shrubbery alone, it was converted to a drug sanitarium before it burned to the ground in 1908. From Polk's Seattle City Directory, *1909; Courtesy of University of Washington Library*

The University of Washington campus, seen here above and to the right of the gas works on Lake Union, was beginning to show the outlines of its present configuration in this 1910 photograph by Webster and Stevens. Some buildings remain from the AYP. The Latona and University bridges can be seen against the far shore in front of the University District. With the arrival of the natural gas pipeline, the gas works was no longer needed to transform coal into heating gas. The tank still stands, but the site is now a city park. Photo by Webster and Stevens; courtesy of Lou Miller

16636
W&S

The old Skid Road area, near the street down which oxen dragged the first logs to Yesler's mill, was sometimes called South of the Slot (a reference to the cable line that climbed the hill), Down on the Sawdust, White Chapel, the Tenderloin, or the Restricted District. It offered sin-on-the-second-floor in establishments of minimal glamor. Some boasted of a French connection, others promised gaiety, one entrepreneur with a bent for honesty called his, quite simply, the Red Light. The photo was taken from Fifth and King streets, circa 1905. Courtesy of Washington State Library

The oldest profession might not change, but the police, starting in 1906, made their appointed rounds in their first patrol van with internal combustion. The picture was taken in front of the old Katzenjammer House city hall. Courtesy of Seattle Public Library

Cartoonists loved Hi Gill. He was so thin that Wilson Mizner, a celebrated wit of the Gold Rush era, defined him as "a trellis for varicose veins." This cartoon from Argus Magazine is one of the few that did not show him with the corn cob pipe he always carried but seldom smoked. Courtesy of Photograph Collection, University of Washington Library

Harper's Weekly gave national publicity to this picture of "the largest brothel in the world." It was built partly on a city street, Tenth Avenue South, by friends of the Gill Administration, with accommodations for 250 girls. The foundation of another building, even larger and also extending onto the street, had been built by the time the newly enfranchised women of Seattle dis-elected the mayor. The second building was never completed. The first was turned into a rooming house which was destroyed in August 1951 when a Boeing bomber crashed into it. Photograph from Harper's Weekly, 1914; courtesy of Photograph Collection, University of Washington Library

Seattle police smashed up a drug store suspected of selling alcohol during Hi Gill's two-year impersonation of a reform mayor. Courtesy of Photograph Collection, University of Washington Library

Purchase of the twenty-acre Smith Cove site from the Great Northern Railroad for $150,000 was one of the first projects undertaken by the Port of Seattle after its formation in 1911. Construction of the first Port of Seattle pier (later called Pier 40 and now known as Pier 90) began on July 17, 1914. Half a mile long and a city block in width, it was when completed the largest pier on the Pacific coast. Piers 90 and 91 still share the honor of being the longest earth-filled piers in the United States. Courtesy of Port of Seattle

Dedication of the Bell Street Terminal "recreation roof" in 1915. The port commission worked with the Seattle Parks Commission to establish the public park on top of their new four-story combination office, warehouse, and cold storage depot at Pier 66. The roof supported a solarium, a salt water pool, and a Happy Land, where parents could leave children while shopping at the Pike Place Market nearby. The Terminal Building still houses the port's administrative offices, but the recreation roof has been closed since the 1920s. Officials said it became a rendezvous for sailors and prostitutes to the exclusion of respectable families. In 1977 a public waterfront park, without child care service, was established a few blocks south. Courtesy of Port of Seattle

Members of the Puget Sound Fisheries Association Committee were on hand for the dedication of Fisherman's Terminal in 1914. A man might get by without a mustache but not without a hat. Left to right: E. Hoen, August F. Rudene, Severin Z. Watney, O. R. Woog, Benjamin Enerson, Adolf Jacobson, Carl Halls, C. Nelson and Charles Issakson. Photograph by Kneisle; courtesy of Inga Nelson Stangvik

Will Hudson, a Pathe News *photographer, caught this picture of a netful of big ones in 1918. Courtesy of Jean Hudson Lunzer*

From a postcard; courtesy of Photograph Collection, University of Washington Library

The Spokane Street Terminal's cold storage warehouse was stacked to the rafters with frozen fish when this photo was taken about 1920. The Port of Seattle started building the facility in 1914 to provide an alternative to expensive private operations. Construction was delayed by a court challenge from private dock and wharf owners, but the warehouse was completed in time to help Seattle dominate West Coast shipping during World War I. Courtesy of Port of Seattle

The S.S. Swinomish of the United States Engineering Department was the first vessel to pass through the Hiram Chittenden Locks when they were completed in 1916, but the formal first passage was attributed to the S.S. Roosevelt, which had been the vessel used by Admiral Robert Peary for his North Pole expedition in 1909. Photograph by Asahel Curtis; courtesy of Photograph Collection, University of Washington Library

Lake Washington and Lake Union were still called by their Indian names of Hyas Chuck and Tenas Chuck ("Big Water" and "Little Water") when Captain George B. McClellan suggested in an 1853 report to the secretary of war that if connected by a canal to Elliott Bay they would "form the finest naval resort in the world."

Harvey Pike's efforts to dig a canal between the lakes failed. They were connected by a narrow channel in the 1870s, but it was 1916 before the last cut was made. Lake Washington dropped eight feet as its water drained into Lake Union then out through the Chittenden locks. The lowering of the lake meant that its Black River outlet simply dried up.

Adding Lake Union and Lake Washington to the area available for ocean-going ships increased Seattle's waterfront to 193 miles. Photograph by Asahel Curtis; courtesy of Seattle Public Library

Shipment of logs to Japan, now a controversial practice because of its effect on lumber industry jobs and prices, began during World War I. (Finished lumber exports to Japan had risen dramatically in the 1890s when that nation, which was industrializing, overcut its forests.) The logs floating by the tracks are part of an order from Suzuki & Company for 2,600 fir pilings, sixty to seventy-two feet long. Photograph by K. Kiyota; courtesy of Port of Seattle

Laura Kiehl, studying her dance program before an Alpha Gamma Delta formal, was graduated from the University of Washington in 1916. Unable to find work in any Seattle brokerage house because of her sex, she obtained a brokerage license of her own, the first issued to a woman in the state. For years her office was in the Smith Building. She died in January 1982, aged ninety-two. Photograph by H. Ambrose Kiehl; courtesy of Laura Kiehl

The Smith Building dominated the business district for fifty years after its completion in 1914 and was a source of community pride from the October day in 1910 when the Times devoted most of its front page to a colored picture of the planned structure and described it in a sentence nearly as long as the building would be tall:

Forty-two stories high, the tallest building in the United States outside of New York and the third highest mercantile building in the world in linear feet, with a huge glass ball inclosing an electric flash light surmounting its tower at a height of 467 feet from the street level, with glistening walls of cream colored brick on the main building and pure white tiling on the exterior of its twenty-two story tower, the magnificent L. C. Smith Building, to be erected at the northeast corner of Second Avenue and Yesler Way, at an estimated cost of $1,500,000, will make Seattle remarkable all over the country in the matter of commercial buildings and furnish the city with a landmark that will fix itself upon the memory of visitors from all over the United States.

Photograph by Webster and Stevens; courtesy of John and Lael Hanawalt, Old Seattle Paperworks

Nellie Cornish set up shop with a group of music teachers in 1914. The first home of the Cornish School ws in the Booth Building at Broadway and East Pine, shown here. In 1921 the school moved to its present site at Harvard and East Roy. Neighbors sued to have Cornish closed as a public nuisance, but Judge A. W. Frater suggested that the plaintiffs move out of town if they didn't care for urban noises. The Booth Building is now occupied by the Burnley School of Professional Art. Photograph by C. F. Todd; courtesy of Photograph collection, University of Washington Library

The electric cars now making a modest comeback in Seattle are a far cry from this elegant model. The house in the background is the Rhodes Mansion, built in 1911 and still standing at 1901 Tenth Avneue East. Courtesy of John and Lael Hanawalt, Old Seattle Paperworks

The policeman still was on horseback in 1912, but the candidate of the Progressive Party, Theodore Roosevelt, campaigned au courant in a horseless carriage. Photograph by Will Hudson; courtesy of Jean Hudson Lunzer

An electric car crackup. Courtesy of John and Lael Hanawalt, Old Seattle Paperworks

New vistas were opening for the tourist. By 1913 it was possible to get to The Mountain by carriage. Photograph by Will Hudson; courtesy of Jean Hudson Lunzer

Getting through the Cascades was still difficult. Drivers in the transcontinental race of 1909 declared Snoqualmie Pass the worst hazard they faced between New York and Seattle, and it was "no bargain" in 1915. Courtesy of John and Lael Hanawalt, Old Seattle Paperworks

There was a road from Fort Lawton down to the beach near the West Point lighthouse. The ladies often went there for picnics while the men were working. Photograph by H. Ambrose Kiehl; courtesy of Laura Kiehl

A family picnic in Kinnear Park, not far from the bandstand, in the summer of 1913. Photograph by Ambrose Kiehl; courtesy of Laura Kiehl

An outing to Bryn Mawr at the south end of Lake Washington, about 1914. Photograph by H. Ambrose Kiehl; courtesy of Laura Kiehl

Three generations of Makah Indians from Neah Bay sold baskets at a downtown corner in 1916, a common sight until the 1920s. Photograph by Asahel Curtis; courtesy of Photograph Collection, University of Washington Library

Boosters spent months planning the 1913 Golden Potlatch, the 50th anniversary of the annual summer Potlatch Days honoring Seattle's pioneers. But the most memorable event was impromptu. Incited by inflammatory editorials protesting the presence in the parade of what the Seattle Times considered "red-flag worshippers and anarchists," a mob wrecked the headquarters of the Industrial Workers of the World on Washington Street, demolished a news stand at Fourth and Pike, and raided the I.W.W. office in the Nestor Building on Westlake as well as two Socialist halls in the Granite Hotel at Fifth and Virginia and an old church at Seventh and Olive. The Times reported in a news story the next day.

The smashing of chairs and tables, the rending of yielding timbers, the creaking and groaning of sundered walls, and above the rest the crash of glass of the windows on the east side all blended together in one grand Wagnerian cacaphony. And all the while the crowd outside just howled and cheered. It was almost more joy than they could stand.

Spectators posed in front of a burned piano taken from the Socialist hall at Seventh and Olive. Photographs by Asahel Curtis; courtesy of Photograph Collections, University of Washington Library

Seattle's love affair with the airplane began with the visit in March 1910 of Charles Hamilton to the Meadows, the race track which operated on today's Boeing Field. Hundreds cheered as he maneuvered his flimsy biplane at speeds estimated at sixty miles an hour. Hamilton stalled over Meadows Lake and ended his flight in the water, but was rescued. Observed the Argus: "Girls, if you marry for money pick an old man or an aviator." Photographs by Asahel Curtis; courtesy of Photograph Collection, University of Washington Library

The seven-story Lincoln Hotel at the northwest corner of Fourth and Madison was built in 1900 and destroyed by fire in 1920. It offered fine views of the bay, the Olympics, and the Cascades from the elegant garden on its roof. The Carnegie Library stood across Fourth Avenue. Courtesy of Seattle Public Library

On July 4, 1914, William E. Boeing, heir to a Midwest lumber and iron fortune, and Conrad Westervelt, a former navy lieutenant, took their first flights over Lake Washington in a pusher-prop hydroplane piloted by Terah Maroney. They liked the experience but decided they could build a better plane. Two years later their first B & W (for

Boeing and Westervelt) made its test flight from a hangar on Lake Union. The 1916 plane, shown here, had a wing span of 52 feet, was 27 feet 6 inches long, and weighed 2,800 pounds. Its 125-horsepower Hall Scott engine could propel it at 75 miles an hour. Courtesy of Boeing Company

The scene looks more Mediterranean than Puget Sound, but the photograph was taken in Seattle on the roof of the Lincoln Hotel. Photograph by Webster and Stevens; courtesy of Oregon Historical Society

Looking down First Avenue from Pine Street during the February 1916 snow. The Liberty Theatre sign levitates above the banked-up snow on the left, and the Corner Market Building is recognizable on the right. Photograph by C. F. Todd; courtesy of Photograph Collection, University of Washington Library

Ice skating on Green Lake in 1916. Skating is still a popular, though forbidden, activity during Seattle's rare hard freezes. The lake was larger and shallower at that time. Originally a remnant of a glacially formed drainage system, it began silting up long before humans appeared on the scene. The big change in the lake, however, came after it was acquired by the city in 1905. The Olmsted Brothers recommended a major fill to create a new shoreline. In the course of this work the outlet to the Ravenna ravine was closed. Soon after, the lake turned a much richer green. Now fresh water is pumped through daily. Photographs by Max Loudon; courtesy of Grace Loudon McAdam and Old Seattle Paperworks

168

An elephant led the parade past the Maynard Building on the northwest corner of First and Washington when the circus came to town in 1917. The building has been renovated and still stands in 1982. Photograph by Max Loudon; courtesy of Grace Loudoun McAdam and John and Lael Hanawalt, Old Seattle Paperworks

They were getting ready to raise the big top on the present site of the Seattle Center. Fourth Avenue is on the right. Photographer Max Loudon was standing at about Thomas. Courtesy of Grace Loudon McAdam and John and Lael Hanawalt, Old Seattle Paperworks

Grace Loudon (left) and Edith Olson, who worked at the Bon Marche, were extras when the Russian Ballet danced Cleopatra *in Seattle on February 17, 1917. Here they pose outside the Metropolitan Theater (since demolished) before the Olympic Hotel was built around it. Photograph by Max Loudon; courtesy of Grace Loudon McAdam*

The cast of Chu Chin Chow, *one of the great hits of the war years, posed outside the Metropolitan Theater in the spring of 1917. Oscar Asche's musical was based on the* Arabian Nights. *That's*

Ali Baba surrounded by middle eastern maidens. One of the songs, popular at the Pike Street Market, began with the lines: "Here be oysters stewed in honey, and conger eels cooked in snow." James

Beard credits it with stirring his interest in sweet and sour cooking. Photograph by Max Loudon; courtesy of Grace Loudon McAdam

Electricity was cheap in Seattle, and modern living demanded a festoon of cords on the dining room table, a switchboard on the wall. This picture was taken on March 28, 1917, at the residence of Burton and Ruth Stare, 802 Thirty-second Avenue. Mr. Stare was president of the Northwestern Supply Company. Photograph by James P. Lee; courtesy of Photograph Collection, University of Washington Library

The Weisfield chain had its start with a store at 304 Union Street in 1917. Ralph Goldberg and Sam Weisfield stand in front. Courtesy of Photograph Collection, University of Washington Library

As late as 1918 some Teamsters still drove teams. These horses were hauling coal for the Seattle Fuel Company. Photograph by James P. Lee, June 29, 1918; courtesy of Photograph Collection, University of Washington Library

Three Seattle favorites are caught in this photo from 1917. The Smith Tower was still the tallest building west of the Mississippi. The clock tower on the Colman Dock told travelers whether the boats had met their schedule. The steamer H. B. Kennedy, *which later became the ferry* Seattle, *took part in the rescue of passengers after the runaway* Yosemite *was wrecked in Port Orchard Bay in 1909 and when the steamer* Tolo *and the tug* Magic *collided between Alki Point and Bainbridge Island in 1917. Courtesy of Seattle Public Library*

Seattle boomed during the years of American participation in the First World War. It was a time of parades, prosperity, employment, and manifesta- tions of patriotism. It's not hard to guess who bought the bond in this group. Courtesy of John and Lael Hanawalt, Old Seattle Paperworks

One of the delights of bathing at Alki Point was the surf kicked up by the passage of the Tacoma and the Indianapolis on their trips between Tacoma and Seattle. Photograph by Asahel Curtis; courtesy of Photograph Collection, University of Washington Library

The Industrial Workers of the World, whose Marxist rhetoric and opposition to the war made them targets of the press, the justice department, and much of the public, also gained membership. Here members and supporters posed at a Class War Picnic held on July 20, 1917, to raise money for a legal defense fund. The picnic attracted a wholesome looking crowd and a notably fashionable blonde, at right, but did not still public doubts about the Wobblies. Courtesy of Pacific Northwest Labor History Association

During the war, women workers of the Bon Marche wrapped bandages and sewed nightgowns. They didn't wear nurses' uniforms except when called on to parade. Photograph by Max Loudon; courtesy of Grace Loudon McAdam

Nuns of the Columbus Sanitarium (now Cabrini Hospital) posed during the First World War. Photograph by Max Loudon; courtesy of Grace Loudon McAdam

A month after the first B & W was tested in 1916, William Boeing incorporated Pacific Aero Products Company "to manufacture airplanes or other products, to operate a flying school, and to act as a common carrier of passengers and freight by aerial navigation." Soon after the United States entered World War I, the name was changed to the Boeing Airplane Company. Boeing set out after military contracts. The first one was with the navy for fifty Model C versions of the B & W. They were built in the Red Barn, the former E. C. Heath shipyard on the Duwamish, which young Boeing had bought earlier in order to build a yacht. With the plant working on military orders, sentries were stationed to challenge visitors. Photograph taken June 8, 1917; courtesy of Boeing Company

Schoolchildren joined the war effort and school system photographers recorded their projects. On January 23, 1918, pupils at John Adams sorted sphagnum moss for wound dressings while boys at B. F. Day knitted scarves for soldiers. Other photos taken that day show boxes of trench candles, socks made by more proficient knitters, and a display of 50,000 gun wipes. Courtesy of Seattle Public School Archives

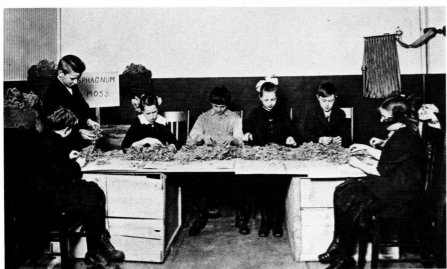

The navy commissioned Boeing to build fifty large flying boats of a type designed by Curtiss, the HS-21, but the German surrender led to the cancellation of the order after only half were completed. Courtesy of Boeing Company

Employees of Stewart & Holmes
Wholesale Drug Company on Third
Avenue between Washington and Main
pose with and without sanitary masks
during the influenza pandemic of 1918.
Photographs by Max Loudon; courtesy of
Grace Loudon McAdam

Armistice Day, 1918. Celebrants piled into and onto a grocery wagon outside the National Bank of Commerce (now Rainier National Bank) at Second and Spring. "We just rode up and down, up and down, shouting and shouting," recalled the photographer. "It was bedlam." Photograph by Grace Loudon McAdam; courtesy of the photographer

After the armistice, employment at Boeing fell from a wartime high of 400 to 80. The company lost $90,000 in 1919. The Post Office had suggested the need for a plane to carry mail, so Boeing set out to design a pusher hydroplane with space behind the pilot for mail bags or two passengers. While the plane was under development, the postmaster of Vancouver, British Columbia, asked if it would be possible to fly some mail from Vancouver to Seattle as a publicity stunt for an exposition. Bill Boeing and test pilot Eddie Hubbard found it an offer they couldn't resist. Using an old Model C, they flew north to Canada (being forced down at Anacortes, en route, by a snowstorm), picked up a mail bag containing sixty letters, and on March 3, 1919, made the return flight of 125 miles from the Royal Vancouver Yacht Club to Lake Union in three hours, including a stop at Edmonds for gas. It was the first international air mail flight. Hubbard is on the left, Boeing on the right. Courtesy of Boeing Company

Union membership in Seattle had increased enormously during the war years, especially among shipyard workers. The owners held cost-plus contracts and were willing to pay high wages. The Federal Fleet Corporation, after initial objections to the pay hikes on the grounds they would force up wages in distant yards, agreed to let them stand when the unions in the Metal Trades Council promised there would be no work stoppages during wartime. Photograph by Max Loudon; courtesy of Grace Loudon McAdam and John and Lael Hanawalt, Old Seattle Paperworks

Ole Hanson, mayor of Seattle from 1918 to 1920, was a real estate salesman who had been elected on a Hate the Hun, Bait the Red platform. The police force, including the detectives shown here, was ordered to be on the alert for subversion, which they saw everywhere. Courtesy of Photograph Collection, University of Washington Library

When the war ended, members of the shipyard unions demanded there be no cut in wages. Charles Piez of the Federal Emergency Trades Council sent a wire to the Metal Trades Association, which was the employers' organization, warning that if they met the union demands the government would cut off their steel allocation. The wire was delivered to the union council instead of the employers' association. On January 21, 1919, the men in the Skinner and Eddy yard walked off the job. Thirty-five thousand men in the other yards followed them. Photograph by Asahel Curtis; courtesy of Photograph Collection, University of Washington Library

U. S. OFFICERS TO DISCUSS STRIKE

The Seattle Star FINAL EDITION

STOP BEFORE IT'S TOO LATE

This is plain talk to the common-sense union men of Seattle.

You are being rushed pell-mell into a general strike. You are being urged to use a dangerous weapon—the general strike, which you have never used before—which, in fact, has never been used anywhere in the United States.

It isn't too late to avert the tragic results that are sure to come from its use.

You men know better than any one else that public sentiment in Seattle—that is, the sentiment of the ninety-five per cent of the people who are not directly involved in the wage dispute of the shipworkers—*is against a general strike.* You know that the general public doesn't think the situation demands the use of that drastic, disaster-breeding move. *You know, too, that you cannot club public sentiment into line, and you know, too, that no strike has ever been won without the moral support of the public.*

The people know that there is a decent solution of the issue at stake. And the issue at stake is merely a better wage to the average unskilled worker in the shipyards. To a large extent public opinion is with these unskilled workers now, but public opinion will turn against them if their wage issue brings chaos and disaster upon the whole community unnecessarily. Seattle today is awake to the fact that she is on the brink of a disaster, *and Seattle is getting fighting mad.* The people are beginning to visualize the horrors that a general tie-up will bring. They see the suffering that is bound to come and *they don't propose to be silent sufferers.*

Today Seattle resents this whole miserable mess. Seattle resents the insolent attitude of the shipyard owners; Seattle resents the verbosity of Director General Piez, whose explanation does not explain; and just as emphatically resents the high-handed "rule or ruin" tactics of the labor leaders who propose to lay the whole city prostrate in a vain attempt to show their power. Let us not mince words. A general strike cannot win unless one of two things happens. Either the ship owners and Piez must yield or else the workers must be able to control the situation *by force.* The latter method is bound to be squelched without much ado, and any decent union men of Seattle will be the sufferers then. *A revolt—and some of your leaders are talking of a revolution—to be successful must have a country-wide application. There isn't a chance to spread it east of the mountains. There isn't a chance to spread it south of Tacoma and today fifty per cent of the unions of Tacoma have turned down the proposition for a general strike.*

Confined to Seattle or even confined to the whole Pacific coast, the use of force by Bolsheviks would be, and should be, quickly dealt with by the army of the United States. These false Bolshevik leaders haven't a chance on earth to win anything for you in this country, *because this country is America—not Russia.*

The strike struck a responsive chord among labor. One after another, members of the smaller Seattle unions, many of them craft-oriented and conservative, voted to hit the bricks in sympathy with the shipyard workers. A general strike was set for ten in the morning, February 6. The Seattle Star *devoted its entire front page on February 4 to an editorial equating the strike with revolution and warning that it was doomed to fail. Courtesy of Photograph Collection, University of Washington Library*

On the day the Star *trumpeted its warning, the most famous editorial in Seattle's history appeared in the Seattle* Union-Record, *the only daily labor paper in the country. It was written by Anna Louise Strong, who was the daughter of the pastor of the Queen Anne Congregational church, the author of* the Power of Prayer, *and a former officer in the Child Welfare Society. Elected to the school board in 1916, Strong was recalled (narrowly) for opposition to the war and the draft. She joined the staff of the* Union-Record. *Her editorial about the strike concluded:*

> We are undertaking the most tremendous move ever made by labor in this country, a move that will lead—No One Knows Where! We do not need hysteria! We need the iron march of labor!

Both editorials were partly right. Labor did not know its destination. The general strike proved that the unions could shut down the city but also demonstrated they had no idea what to do next. The iron march of labor turned into a straggle. The strike was called off, shipyard employment plummeted, and wages were cut.

What followed was bitterness, finger-pointing, defeat of labor candidates in the next elections, and the fading memory of a moment of unity and hope. Courtesy of Photograph Collection, University of Washington Library

Advertisement in a Fleet Week program.
Courtesy of Photography Collection,
University of Washington Library

Woodrow Wilson doffs his silk hat to the crowd. Courtesy of Seattle Public Library

The Atlantic Fleet steamed into Elliott Bay in 1919 as part of a victory cruise. Seattle cheered the great gray battleships and toasted officers and crew at parties ashore, but when President Woodrow Wilson came to visit the fleet, many shipyard workers and their sympathizers turned their backs as his convertible passed. Courtesy of Port of Seattle

"And let the rest of the world go by . . ." Photograph by H. Ambrose Kiehl; courtesy of Laura Kiehl

Chapter **6**

DRIFT AND DEPRESSION

1920-1940

Almost unnoticed was the change in product at Boeing, where between 1920 and 1929 the steamstresses who had fabricated the airplane wings were replaced by metalworkers. Courtesy of Boeing Company

In the 1920s Seattle turned its back on the memories of the war and social causes. Unions lost members and workers lost jobs. Between 1919 and 1929 the number of wage earners employed in manufacturing dropped from nearly 41,000 to 23,000. Seattle drifted, looking for a purpose, its economy kept alive by the professions and the port. It became a waypoint for people and goods headed elsewhere.

The twenties were years of caretaker government, and some of the caretakers proved none too careful about the public weal. Though the university expanded and the Huskies went to the Rose Bowl, culture stagnated. The homefolks cut their lawns, dined in, and went out mainly to the beaches and the mountains.

Seattle, like most cities with a frontier heritage, has always been self-congratulatory, but during the early post-war years it was more proud of what it wasn't than of what it was. Norma Rockliffe, a visitor from Boston, sounded the note Seattle liked to hear in the *Argus Magazine* Christmas Number of December 13, 1924:

There is a tip-toe-ness about Seattle, like a young woman awaiting her lover. And I know who he is, for I've heard her call to him— "Good morning, East!" It will be a good match. When I consider the hot, tired, crowded humans struggling for breath in the concrete fastnesses of the East, and then see these spaces, the rich, untried potentialities of soil and water, then it seems the wedding should be hurried up a bit. She is young, Seattle, but surprisingly old—and wise. I was shocked to find her so stylish and stepping. . . . Boston's Fenway-Riverside Drive can't compare with Lake Washington Boulevard. All the jazz and ritz and bang and zip—and the dignity of a fine

American city has Seattle.

Complacency ended with a crash. The Wall Street debacle of 1929 and the ensuing depression threw thousands out of work. The frail safety net of local welfare institutions collapsed under the strain. In the early thirties a village grew up within the city—Hooverville, a mini-metropolis possessed by the dispossessed.

The state switched from Republican to Democratic, and the left wing of the Democratic party was so strong that Jim Farley, the national chairman, spoke of "the forty-seven states and the Soviet of Washington."

The mid-thirties were marked by bitter strikes as unions fought to organize the basic industries. Jurisdictional war raged between Harry Bridges' longshoremen and Dave Beck's teamsters for control of the warehouses. Seattle papers had denounced Beck as a dangerous radical when he enrolled thousands of new members into the Teamsters, putting himself in a position to control the movement of goods to and from stores and factories, but Harry Bridges, the Australian-born president of the Pacific Coast Longshoremen's Union, made Beck look like a savior to the business community.

The Teamsters controlled the hills, the Longshoremen the beach, and they fought each other for mastery over the men who worked in the warehouses. "Choose me or Bridges," Beck told the bosses, and they chose him. His dominance established, Beck organized other bosses and used the Teamsters as a weapon to guarantee price stability. A grateful establishment responded with marks of appreciation. Beck became president of the University of Washington Board of Regents. When he was elected international president of the Teamsters, the chamber of commerce sent flowers.

May Day ceremonies at the University of Washington. Photograph by Lloyd Linkletter; courtesy of Photograph Collection, University of Washington Library

A summer picnic with a few Occidental faces showing in the background. The annual community picnic held by the Nihon Gakko Japanese school was the biggest event of the summer for the Seattle Japanese community. Weeks of preparation culminated in a day of footraces, Japanese dances, martial arts, hot dogs, pickled rice, fried chicken, and sake—all ending with a baseball tournament.

"The Japanese school picnic was one occasion when every Japanese in the community turned out and all parents bought new clothes for their children," recalled Monica Sone in her autobiography Nisei Daughter. *She continued:*

> *There was a terrific run on children's tennis shoes in the Japanese shoe stores, for the foot races were the most important event of our picnic. All the girls bought snowy-white canvas rubber-soled shoes with a single strap buttoning across the instep and a demure white bow at the toe. The boys wore ankle-high black and white canvas shoes with thick, black rubber soles, guaranteed to transform even a plodding turtle into a bouncing hare.*

Courtesy of Seattle Public Library

185

The shear leg derrick at Smith Cove was the heavy artillery of the port's longshoring arsenal. "Practically all heavy lifts for Japan and Russia are made by this crane," noted the 1921 port Yearbook *in which this photograph appeared. Courtesy of Port of Seattle*

Ten thousand sacks of mail bound for Asia, about to be loaded onto the President Jefferson. *November 28, 1922. Courtesy of Port of Seattle*

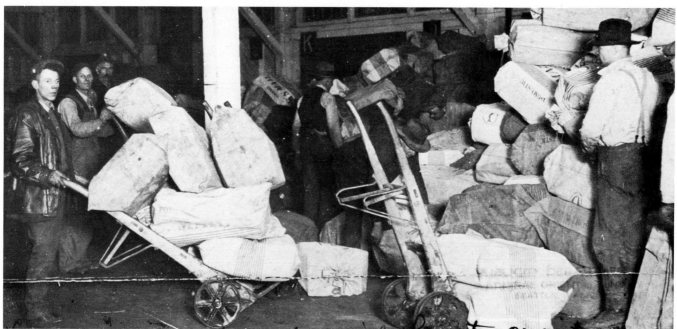

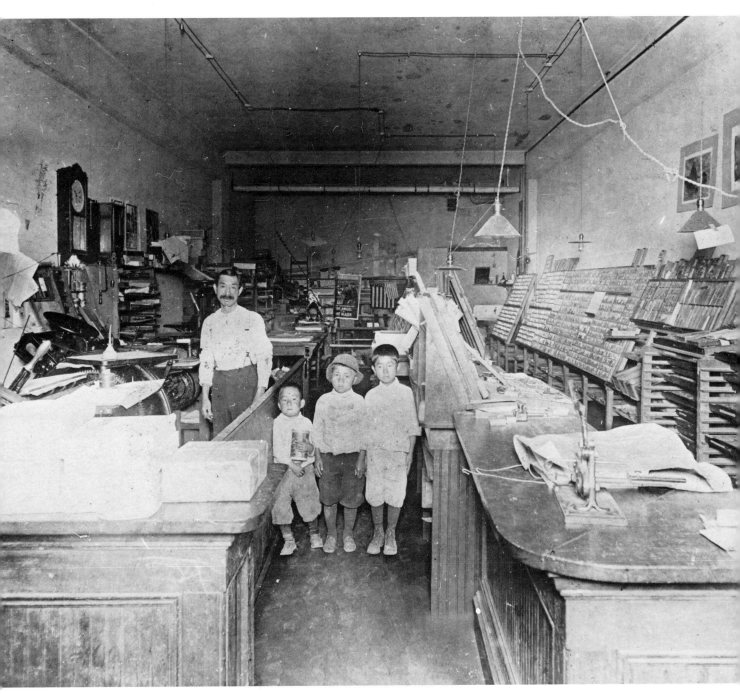

Minosuke Yorita stands with his son, Tats; a friend, Toshi Tsukuno; and an older son, Goro, in the family print shop at 211 Fifth Avenue South. Yorita Printing produced copy in both Japanese and English, which explains the impressive row of typeface boxes along the right wall. Courtesy of Edward and Elizabeth Burke

Seattle politics continued to produce contradictions. The city elected in 1922 and re-elected in 1924 Edwin J. Brown, an advertising dentist ("BEWARE of imitators who use Dr. Brown's name to impose themselves upon unsuspecting persons. . . .") with self-proclaimed socialist tendencies which in practice amounted to himself sharing in the available wealth.

In this photograph in 1923 Vice President Calvin Coolidge and Mayor "Doc" Brown made an odd couple during Silent Cal's stopover in Seattle. *Courtesy of* Seattle Post-Intelligencer

Brown, not the best dressed man in Seattle political history, was caricatured in the June 9, 1924 Post-Intelligencer. *Courtesy of the* Seattle Post-Intelligencer

The town was titillated when Mayor Brown, following the death of his wife, married Anna Lois McTaffe Healy, a showgirl whom the Browns previously had planned to adopt. Courtesy of the Seattle Post-Intelligencer

In 1925, while Doc Brown was away at a convention, the president of the city council served as acting mayor.

The situation was unusual because the council president was a woman, Bertha K. Landes, wife of the dean of the school of science at the University of Washington, and a personality in her own right. "Big Bertha," as the press called her, told the cops to close the town. They said they couldn't because there were a hundred men on the force who had financial interests in nightlife establishments. She said "Fire them."

When Brown got back he hardly recognized the place. In the next election Landes became the first female mayor of an American metropolis. Two years of reform led to the election of Frank Edwards, who promised to refrain from reform.

Bertha Landes, as mayor, continued to make breakfast for her husband, Dean Henry Landes. *Courtesy of the* Seattle Post-Intelligencer

In one of her less controversial actions, the mayor of "She-attle" adjusts the trolley on the first streetcar to move in an experiment with low-cost downtown fares. *Courtesy of the* Seattle Post-Intelligencer

189

A work party on the field at Memorial Stadium, now on the grounds of the Seattle Center. The Civic Auditorium behind the field was an object of community self-congratulation when it was finished in 1928, but by the time planners for the Seattle World's Fair looked it over thirty years later it was described as "a flagrantly barn-like edifice whose enigmatic vistas and erratic acoustics had long been the curse of the local lovers of ballet and music." On the advice of architect Minoru Yamasaki, the auditorium was not abandoned. Instead, it was gutted and redone as the present Opera House. Courtesy of Port of Seattle

Throughout the changes of the 1920s, the beaches retained their appeal. Seattle was not yet a restaurant town. When people ate out, they usually picnicked. Photograph by H. Ambrose Kiehl, courtesy of Laura Kiehl

*A new Boeing appeared over Lake
Washington in 1930, the Monomail.
This one-place, open-cockpit, low-wing
mail plane was the first truly revo-
lutionary Boeing plane—the first ex-
pression of what became the Boeing
design philosophy. It was the first all-
metal airplane of monocoque construction, the type in which the covering
absorbs much of the stress to which the
body is subjected. Seward Park lies
below the plane. Courtesy of Boeing
company*

A new neighborhood took shape in the early 1930s. Its residents called it Hooverville in honor of the president on whom they blamed the miseries caused by the Wall Street crash of 1929 and the ensuing depression. The community sprang up just west of the present site of the Kingdome. Housing in Hooverville ranged from roofed dugouts and refurbished packing crates to a cottage, built by an unemployed carpenter, that had a kitchen, dining room, two bedrooms, a storeroom, and even a front porch.

Of 632 men living in Hooverville when a graduate student at the University of Washington took an informal census in 1934, 11 percent had never attended school and 88 percent had gotten no farther than the eighth grade. Only five had been graduated from college. Another five had taken some classes. Of the ten college men, four were Filipinos. Seven women lived in Hooverville. Photograph by James P. Lee; courtesy of Pacific Northwest Labor History Association and the Photography Collection, University of Washington Library

Be it ever so humble—a converted packing case was better than no home at all. Photograph by James P. Lee, October 27, 1931; courtesy of Pacific

Northwest Labor History Association and the Photograph Collection, University of Washington Library

This spiffy gent hadn't had time to wear out his Sunday clothes before he found himself living in a shack of canvas and tin. Photograph by James P. Lee; courtesy of Photograph Collection, University of Washington Library

Dave Beck, Teamster—
Hell, the day when there was
unrestricted competition with no
regulation is long gone. You don't
think so, you go downtown and
buy a plane ticket to Chicago and
see how unrestricted competition
on plane tickets is. But I don't
raise the cost of living and there's
no damn truth to saying we
pyramid the cost of living.
Courtesy of Seattle Post-Intelligencer

Harry Bridges, Longshoreman—
We take the stand that we as
workers have nothing in common
with the employers. We are in a
class struggle, and we subscribe to
the belief that if the employer is
not in business his products will
still be necessary and we will still
be providing them when there is
no employing class. We frankly
believe that day is coming.
Courtesy of Seattle Post-Intelligencer

Mass picketing marked the prolonged 1934 maritime workers' strike, which tied up most ports on the Pacific Coast. Here, strikers and their sympathizers prevent the loading of the Alaska Streamship Company's liner Victoria on May 15. Five weeks later, mounted police swinging billy clubs charged a crowd at Pier 40 when it refused to move for a locomotive. The Post-Intelligencer reported three strikers' heads were "broken" in the clash. Courtesy of Seattle Post-Intelligencer

The Teamsters provided crucial support for the American Newspaper Guild in its 1936 strike against the Seattle Post-Intelligencer, causing the Seattle Times to editorialize that city government rested "in the firm hands of Dave Beck and his brawny crew," and to warn that "suspension of the Post-Intelligencer is more likely than not to mark the place where Seattle lies—dead." Courtesy of Pacific Northwest Labor History Association

Beck sold himself to the business community as a labor leader who understood the profit motive: "We recognize that labor cannot receive a fair wage unless business receives a just profit on its investment," he told the chamber of commerce. Here he brightens the day for Sydney R. Imus, assistant vice president and manager of the Sea-First Sixth and Denny branch, by depositing $1 million, the largest new deposit in the branch's brief history. Courtesy of Seattle Post-Intelligencer

Mayor John Dore was another of Seattle's political quick change artists. First elected on a cut-the-costs-and-reduce-the-taxes program, Dore trimmed the budget, fired everybody not nailed in by civil service, kept the city in the black at the bottom of the Depression, and lost the next election when the business community supported somebody else. He ran again two years later as the candidate of labor, especially the Teamsters, most especially Dave Beck. "Brother Beck was the greatest factor in my election," he told the state American Federation of Labor (AFL) convention in 1936, "and I say again that I am going to pay back my debt to Dave Beck and the Teamsters, regardless of what happens." Here Dore addresses the National Unemployed Council at City Hall Park. Courtesy of University of Washington Library

A survey of the social and economic condition of Seattle blacks was conducted by a black task force funded by the state of Washington in 1934. Courtesy of Photograph Collection, University of Washington Library

Seattle City Light Superintendent J. D. Ross (center) is back on the ground after inspecting a tower at the Diablo Dam site in 1935. With him are Bill Murtha, Dan Campbell, Frank Fitts, and Larry Maddock. Seattle was expanding its sources of hydroelectricity in hopes of attracting new industry. Courtesy of Seattle City Light

A Seattle City Light substation makes the method message clear: Plenty of power, and it's cheap. Courtesy of Seattle City Light

Shisui Mujashita conducted members of the Seattle Symphony; a Japanese chorus; and Sachika Ochin, pianist, in a performance of his own works at the Nippon Kan Theatre on May 8, 1936. Courtesy of Edward and Elizabeth Burke

May Sasaki (right) and a companion from the Ihara family perform a Kabuki story dance in the Nippon Kan Theatre in the late 1930s. The forced relocation of Japanese families after Pearl Harbor disrupted the close-knit Japanese community. The Ihara girl returned with her family to Japan; the Sasakis were sent to a concentration camp. Built by the Japanese community in 1910, the Nippon Kan also fell into disuse during the war. It has recently been restored through efforts led by Edward and Elizabeth Burke and in 1981 was once again the scene of a Kabuki performance. Courtesy of Edward and Elizabeth Burke and May Sasaki

Imagine taking a vessel that had a reputation as a jinx ship, that had been gutted by fire and left idle for eight years, and turning it into the most popular vessel on the sound. That was the public relations triumph performed by the Black Ball Line when it bought the hulk of the former San Francisco Bay ferry Peralta, had it towed to Seattle, and rebuilt it with a superstructure of steel painted to look like aluminum. They renamed her Kalakala, which means "flying bird" in Salish, and billed her as the world's only streamlined ferry, then put her on the run to Bremerton. She was a home away from home for thousands of Seattle workers who commuted to the naval shipyard during the war. Courtesy of Photograph Collection, University of Washington Library

Cruisers and rowboats lined up on the waterfront in the late 1930s. Courtesy of Port of Seattle

Dwight Long became a local hero when he sailed the Seattle-built Idle Hour around the world, alone. It took him four years. Long wrote a book, Seven Seas on a Shoestring, and organized a film company, Shoestring Pictures, Inc. Photograph by Will Hudson' courtesy of Jean Hudson Lunzer

University of Washington crews dominated rowing in the 1930s, sweeping the Poughkeepsie regatta three times and winning the Olympic gold at Berlin in 1936. Coach Al Ulbrickson, here supervising a workout in the Barge, was mentioned as a possibility for governor. Photograph by Will Hudson; courtesy of Jean Hudson Lunzer

The steam permanent wave machines of the 1930s give a horror movie touch to this photo publicizing one of the vocational training programs offered at Edison School. The school district's annual report for 1938 also made note of Edison's courses in home economics for boys planning careers as chefs, in home management for motherless girls, and in "physical hardening" for an unspecified clientele. Courtesy of Seattle Public Schools Archives

Spring fever—
    Lincoln High School students stage a street dance on May 21, 1940. In 1981, despite pleas from parents, teachers, students and alumni, the Seattle School Board voted to include *Lincoln in a wave of school closures, and in June the students filed out through its doors for the last time.*
Courtesy of Wallingford Community Council

The B-17 was the basic bomber in the early years of the war. This is model B-17G. Courtesy of Boeing Company

Chapter 7

THE YEARS OF BOEING BOOM

1940-1968

It is hard to remember that when World War II began in 1939, the Boeing Company (then still called the Boeing Airplane Company) did not dominate the Seattle economy. Boeing employed about 4,000 workers—one of every five then working at manufacturing in King County; most were engaged in fabricating planes on a subcontract for the Douglas Company of California.

After the British retreat from Dunkirk and the start of the Luftwaffe blitz, England placed orders with Boeing for a large precision bomber the company had developed in the mid-1930s—the B-17, or Flying Fortress. A year after German tanks entered Poland, Boeing employment had increased to 20,000; by the time of Pearl Harbor, to 30,000; and after President Roosevelt called on U.S. industry to turn out 50,000 planes a year—more aircraft than had been built world-wide since the Wright Brothers' first flight—employment passed 50,000.

Boeing's sales in 1944, the peak war year, stood at $600 million, seven times the value of all Seattle manufactured goods in the last peacetime year. But what would happen when peace broke out? Would cutbacks at Boeing trigger the type of reaction that the layoffs in the shipyards had caused in 1919?

In September of 1945, the month Japan surrendered, William M. Allen, a corporation lawyer in the firm of Holman, Sprague and Allen, took over as president of the company. On the same day the government terminated most of its orders for B-29 Superfortress bombers. A shudder ran through the economy as Allen cut employment to 11,000 and sales for 1946 fell to a piddling $14 million, little more than 2 percent of the wartime high.

Allen held his corps of engineers and key workers together by producing, at a loss, a post-war version of the civilian Stratocruiser. He fought off (with the help of the Teamsters' Dave Beck) the demands of the Aero-Mechanics union in a major strike. He thus bought time until the cold war with the Soviet Union and the hot war with Korea brought orders from the Pentagon for a new generation of jet bombers, the B-47s and later the B-52s.

Boeing prospered, as did Seattle, but again from a wartime economy. In 1952 Allen gambled the company's entire reserves on a civilian venture, the creation of a commercial jet transport to be called the 707. It took seven years to apply bomber technology to passenger-plane use, but the gamble paid off. The 707 changed the patterns of air travel, dominated the world market for long-range commercial airliners, and produced profits that enabled Boeing to develop the short-range 727, the medium 737 and then the mammoth 747, a plane

with a fuselage longer than the distance covered by the Kitty Hawk flight.

By 1959 Boeing employed 58,000—one out of every two workers engaged in manufacturing in King County. Seattle was booming. Civic leaders decided to throw another party to call attention to their success. They called it Century 21. It drew 9,609,969 persons, it ended in the black, and it left the city with the Opera House, Playhouse, Science Center and, what has become the symbol of Seattle, the Space Needle.

Then the Boeing boom collapsed. The company had undertaken the creation of a supersonic transport—the SST—at the same time it was developing the 747. Employment surged past the 100,000 mark. But the predicted geometric growth in air travel failed to materialize. Sales of 747s tapered off. Congress voted against continuing support for the development of the supersonic prototype. Boeing employment fell by half, Seattle unemployment rose to twice the national average, and a charity called Neighbors in Need was formed to help high-priced professionals with split level houses, big mortgages, no income, and no buyers.

Someone put on a billboard: "Will the last person leaving Seattle please turn out the lights."

A corporation lawyer with no engineering experience, William M. Allen was forty-five years old when he became president of the Boeing Company at the moment the Pentagon terminated production of the B-29 bomber. He guided Boeing into age of commercial jet transportation with his gamble on the 707 jetliner. Courtesy of Argus Magazine

Now you see it . . . .

Now you don't . . . .
The giant Plant II on the Duwamish was considered an inviting target for a Japanese bombing attack, so it was concealed under the world's largest tent. Courtesy of Boeing Company

An off-duty stenographer strolls through the make-believe garden. Courtesy of Boeing Company

V-J Day. Mrs. C. R. Gresham (front) and Mrs. Dorothy Hreha scan the Post-Intelligencer *war extra edition on Japan's surrender at a coffee shop counter. Courtesy of the* Seattle Post-Intelligencer

Last days of the small-town airport: Sea-Tac passenger terminal in 1947. Courtesy of Port of Seattle

Dedication ceremonies for the main passenger terminal at Sea-Tac on July 9, 1949. The original appropriation for the project, in 1942, was $600,000. Costs had risen to $11 million by the time this picture was taken, and another $200 million plus has been spent since. Nevertheless, Sea-Tac has been a money maker. Courtesy of the Port of Seattle

The opening of Northgate in 1949 inaugurated the shopping center era for Seattle. The suburban fringes of North Seattle shown in this photo promptly filled in with homes and businesses. Courtesy of Photograph Collection, University of Washington Library

The jet technology that went into the heavy bombers made possible the Boeing 707 Jet Stratoliners, America's first commercial jets. The top plane is the first production 707, which made its maiden flight December 20, 1957. Below it is the third production 707. New Boeing designs cause occasional traffic jams as I-5 commuters slow to see the latest in aviation engineering on the runway at Boeing Field. Courtesy of Boeing Airplane Company

As a young man in Seattle Mark Tobey taught at the Cornish School and painted ducks for a stage setting at twenty-five cents a bird. By the 1950s, though no longer a resident, he was claimed as the most prominent member of the Northwest School of painting. Photograph by Johsel Namkung; courtesy of the photographer

A make-believe totem pole starts on its way to Seattle's sister port of Kobe, Japan, around 1959. This thoroughly unauthentic carving was replaced a few years later by a larger, more skillfully carved totem, the work of Lummi carver Joe Hillaire. The pole now stands in a Kobe park. Pictured are the acting Japanese consul, Port Commissioner Ed Savage, Mayor Gordon Clinton in the foreground, and a Northwest Airline flight attendant. Courtesy of Port of Seattle.

Dave Beck's reign as Seattle's dominant citizen ended with his conviction in Federal Judge George Boldt's court on charges of income tax evasion. His appeals exhausted, Beck, accompanied by United States Deputy Marshall Dick

Osborn, boards the boat at Steilacoom for the voyage to the federal penitentiary on McNeil Island in 1959. *Courtesy of* Seattle Post-Intelligencer *and Associated Press*

Seattle loved Mark Tobey for his work on Northwest themes more than for the later abstractions that won first prize of the Commune of Venice at the XXIX Biennale. This 1941 watercolor, "Rummage," was one of the major works in a series he painted on the Pike Place Market, which he described in The World of a Market *(University of Washington Press)* as "a refuge, an oasis, a most human growth, the heart and soul of Seattle." *From Seattle Art Museum*

The Science Center stands against the vista of Smith's Cove, Magnolia Bluff and, across the sound, the Olympic Mountains. *Courtesy of Photograph Collection, University of Washington Library*

Century 21 not only paid all of its bills but left Seattle with the Monorail (foreground) connecting the fairgrounds with downtown, the Space Needle (right), the Coliseum for sporting events and exhibitions (center), and the Science Center and Arches of Science (left). Courtesy of Photograph Collection, University of Washington Library

City Councilman Al Rochester (right), whose soliloquy on the wonders of the Alaska Yukon Pacific exposition is quoted on page 104, was a leading advocate of the 1962 World's Fair. He insisted that it should be "something special, not just another showcase for the state seal done in corn tassels, milk cans and steers' rears." Senator Warren G. Magnuson, standing beside Rochester, managed to tack a $9,000,000 supplemental appropriation for the fair onto a multi-billion dollar bill dear to the Pentagon's heart. Looking on as Al and Maggie discuss a model of the fair grounds are John Haydon (left), port commissioner and publisher of the Marine Digest, *and Roy Peterson, district director of customs. Courtesy of Port of Seattle*

The fair ended but festivals continued. Seafair, an annual week of civic self-promotion inaugurated in 1949 as a sequel to the Potlatch Days, culminates with world class hydroplane races on Lake Washington. The merits of the rooster tails are debated anew each summer as Seafair approaches, and the lakeside residents who bear the brunt of the noise, traffic, and monumental trash piles left by the fans keep hoping that their allure will eventually fade. So far, the hundreds of thousands of spectators who jam the shore at race time have remained enthusiastic. *Photograph by Forde Photographers; author's collection*

In spite of houseboats, sailboats, canoes, and swimmers, Lake Union is still working water. Courtesy of Argus *Magazine*

The pleasure boating season officially starts the first Sunday in May when a parade of decorated boats with well-stocked galleys heads through the Montlake Cut to spend the day socializing on Lake Washington. In fact, boaters are out in all seasons, and sailboat races are held even in the snow. Courtesy of Bruce Brown

Downtown interests still felt it helped business to route all possible traffic through the business district. Suggestions that the new interstate highway run to the east of Lake Washington were not heeded. A giant bridge was built to carry north-south traffic across Lake Union. Courtesy of Seattle Public Library

This picture of a closed beach on Lake Washington was one of the most effective weapons in the campaign to create Metro and to end the dumping of raw sewage into what Seattle had once boasted of as "a mountain lake at sea level." Photograph courtesy of Metro, Municipality of Metropolitan Seattle

Chapter 8

MOST LIVEABLE CITY

1968-1981

The catalyst for change in Seattle city politics was CHECC (Choose an Effective City Council.) The movement took shape in 1966 as an extension of The Group, an informal alliance of well-connected young lawyers, many of whom had been classmates at Harvard. The Group worked on liberal Republican causes and, in meetings usually held at the Athenian Restaurant in the Pike Place Market, brought problems and possible solutions to the attention of liberal journalists in the establishment press. Concentrating on city council races, CHECC helped to elect Phyllis Lamphere, Tim Hill, Sam Smith, Bruce Chapman, and John Miller, all of whom contributed to livelier, more imaginative governance. Some of The Group eventually found the developing CHECC organization too liberal for their taste and parted company. Here the founding members pose on the courthouse portico. Photograph by Mary Randlett; courtesy of Argus Magazine

The Boeing recession proved short-lived. Seattle was not a company town, nor a one-industry town, but a complex organism capable of adapting to changed circumstance.

Roger Sale, in *Seattle, Past to Present,* notes that the response to joblessness was often not flight but craft. "Cottage industries appeared with such profusion that it began to seem that everyone laid off at Boeing had been nursing a secret desire to throw a pot, turn a lathe, cast in metal, or make an omelette." Engineers survived by buying each other's art work. Neighbors in Need found there was neighborliness, and Seattle residents, reminded by recession that experts were not infallible, began to realize that their own judgments, based on knowledge of specific conditions, might be valid. Seattle became cause-oriented. The causes were often single-issue or parochial, but they merged.

The conflicts of Seattle's first century had centered on issues of morals versus money. The civic battles of the late 1960s and the 1970s, however, revealed Seattle as a city conscious that it had a past to preserve and neighborhoods to cherish. When engineers began planning a freeway that would cut between First Hill and downtown, Victor Steinbrueck, architect, professor, and activist, rallied the opposition with sketches of the houses and views that would be lost to progress. Interstate 5 was built through downtown, but the battle was joined. When city government decided to perpetrate urban renewal on the Pike Place Market, transforming it into a parking lot, Steinbrueck called out the troops again. This time he won. Citizen groups then fought off proposals for a third bridge over Lake Washington and a freeway through the arboretum, which would have been named for "That Man Thomson."

Neighborhood consciousness did not mean an end of growth, but it did mean a questioning of most proposed developments. The downtown area sprouted skyscrapers but residential areas clung to their identities.

The contests have produced a healthy tension. Alliances shift as new technologies change the pattern of growth. The old fixation on railroads and highways as guarantors of metropolitan status have faded in the glare of shining office towers and major league teams. The Denny Regrade, which languished for years in its hard won levelness, is sprouting new buildings and new businesses to the dismay of those who had found it a haven of low cost housing.

The 1980s brought reverses. Airlines cancelled orders for Boeing planes and the Pentagon chose Lockheed's C-5Bs over Boeing 747s as military freighters. The university suffered severe budget cuts. Loss of federal and state funds threaten many city programs. Seattle is again in a pause, but in the past each pause has been followed by a lurch in an unexpected direction.

The Sea-First Building goes up at Third and Marion, at one time the site of the Elk's Temple and the Jewish Community Center. Completed in 1968, the fifty-story black tower was immediately nicknamed "the box the Space Needle came in," and, less charitably, "the big ugly." It was the first of a thicket of office towers which have given Seattle a modern metropolitan skyline and have turned some east-west streets into wind tunnels. Courtesy of Argus Magazine

The Port of Seattle's giant grain terminal at Pier 86 is the largest and most efficient in the Northwest. It began operations early in 1970, to the dismay of nearby Queen Anne and Magnolia residents who found it larger, uglier, noisier, and dustier than they had expected. Their feelings were not much soothed by a report from the port that a group of Russian visitors had admired the structure, saying that its gray color blended well with Seattle skies. Photograph by Duff Wilson; courtesy of Argus Magazine

Early days of container shipping featured whirly cranes and containers on the decks of conventional cargo ships. Since 1956, when container shipping began, Seattle has followed the trend, a major reason for the financial success of the port in the last decade. Courtesy of Port of Seattle

215

Even the Space Needle was given a fresh look. Carl Winkelman dangles from a movable platform to clean an out-of-the-way spot. In 1981 it was decided to add a mid-level bulge to make room for another restaurant, which opened in 1982. Photograph by Tom Miller; courtesy of the Tacoma News-Tribune

The murder of Edwin Pratt, civil rights leader and executive director of the Seattle Urban League, underscored the realization that Seattle had not escaped the racial bitterness of the 1960s. Pratt, who like Martin Luther King had angered both conservative whites and militant blacks in his campaigns for open housing and better job opportunities, was gunned down in the doorway of his North Seattle home on January 26, 1969. Two white men were seen driving away from the scene, but no one was ever charged with the crime. The Pratt Fine Arts Center at Twentieth and Yesler and a memorial scholarship fund administered by the Urban League have helped to keep his name alive. Courtesy of Seattle Urban League.

The Vietnam war joined the civil rights movement as a cause of protest in the late 1960s and early 1970s. The University of Washington was the focus for efforts to change government policy, both domestic and foreign. Courtesy of Helix Archive

Protest movements usually flower in urban settings, but the Vietnam generation found it necessary to create a new way to express their rejection of a world they had not made. It was the wilderness festival. Here, thousands find community at Sky River. Courtesy of Humbead Enterprises

The greatest protest demonstration in Seattle's history, more massive than any gathering during the General Strike of 1919, greeted President Nixon's announcement of the extension of the Vietnam fighting into Cambodia. Protestors by the tens of thousands marched down the streets and highways, jamming the Interstate Freeway bridge, carrying banners and counterculture newspapers, and assembling around the federal building under the distress signal of an upside-down flag. Courtesy of Frank B. Denman

The arrival of Chinese premier Deng Xsaioping (also written as Teng Tsaio-Ping) on February 3, 1979, was a three-ring media circus. Generally barred from any actual contact with the diminutive leader of a billion potential consumers, some 200 reporters and news photographers were reduced to covering each other. Deng's visit provoked some anti-communist and pro-Maoist protests, but business leaders, anticipating trade with China, gave him an enthusiastic welcome. "Teng visit to Seattle brings valued customer to Boeing," read one Post-Intelligencer headline, and another front page story was titled "A warm look at Teng humor." Photograph by Charles Nacke; courtesy of Argus Magazine

Seattle City Light Superintendent Gordon Vickery (left) and Mathematical Sciences Northwest consultant Don Shakow, after a 1976 city council meeting. The two men represented opposing philosophies on the increasingly pressing issue of electrical energy. Vickery wanted the city to invest in two nuclear plants to provide the power for future growth. Shakow's study concluded that conservation was a better source of kilowatts. The council eventually sided with Shakow, and the never finished nukes have run up the largest public debt outside the federal government. Photograph by Duff Wilson; courtesy of Argus Magazine

Construction of the Kingdome began in the spring of 1976 on the site of an old railroad yard behind the King Street Station. Now the home of the Mariners, Seahawks, Sonics, Sounders, and events ranging from Billy Graham to Boeing's annual Christmas party, the dome dominates the industrial section south of downtown. A visiting Los Angeles designer suggested that it be enlivened with pink stripes, but Seattleites prefer it sky gray. Courtesy of the Kingdome

Along with a flourishing financial district came the desire for some downtown amenities. Freeway Park, a scaled down and priced up version of an earlier proposal to cover I-5, was opened in 1976 and has become a favored spot for lovers and brown baggers. The park starts at Sixth and Seneca and extends diagonally to Ninth and Union, covering a section of the freeway and masking the sound of traffic with falling water. Photograph by Werner Lenggenhager; courtesy of Washington State Library

219

Rich Beyer with his Thirty-fourth and Fremont landmark, Waiting for the Interurban. *Beyer's eternal commuters have been the subject of gag photos and acts of homage since their installation* in 1978. *Cold weather usually finds them bundled up with donated hats and mufflers. Photograph by Tricia Hines, West Stock, Inc.; courtesy of the photographer and* Fremont Forum

Michael Heizer's sculpture Adjacent,
Against, Upon, *was installed at Myrtle
Edwards Park just north of Pier 70,
December 1976. Paid for with $60,000
in public and private money, the
sculpture went in despite the objections
of Mrs. Edwards' family, who didn't
think the former city councilwoman
would have liked it. Courtesy of* Argus
Magazine

*When the Seattle Supersonics were
leading in the playoffs for the 1978
National Basketball Association championship, the coach of the Washington
Bullets proclaimed "The Opera ain't
over 'til the Fat Lady sings." The
Bullets went on to win that championship. Seattle fans had to wait 'til next
year. But in 1979, when the same two
teams met in the finals, the Fat Lady
sang for the Sonics. Seattle had its first
major league sports championship.
Photograph by Duff Wilson; courtesy of*
Argus Magazine.

Rainer Meidel was named music director and conductor of the Seattle Symphony Orchestra n 1976. Established in 1903 by violinist Harry West, the Symphony has long been prominent in Seattle society life. More recently, it has established itself as a quality orchestra. Photograph by David Medley; courtesy of Seattle Symphony Orchestra

The Seattle Aquarium opened in May 1977 on Piers 59 to 61. It was an immediate hit and grew even more popular with the birth of a sea otter there on May 16, 1979. The youngster became the first surviving sea otter born in captivity, and probably the most carefully watched. Volunteers kept round-the-clock records of his activities. Another otter baby was born in 1980. Courtesy of Seattle Aquarium

The Liu Lin Hai (docked at Pier 91 in foreground) arrived in Seattle April 18, 1979, to load corn. She was the first mainland Chinese ship to enter Elliott Bay in thirty years. Courtesy of Port of

For Sale signs on boats at Fisherman's Terminal in 1977 testify to hard times in the commercial salmon fishery. Overfishing and destruction of salmon habitat have made it hard for both white and Indian fishermen to make a living at their traditional occupation— and salmon, a pioneer staple, has become a luxury food. Photograph by Bruce Brown; courtesy of Argus Magazine

The days of the regrades are over, but Seattle is still rearranging its topography. The Port of Seattle's Terminal 37-46 complex replaced old piers (including the old Washington Tug and Barge installation at Pier 43) with fill and built a horizontal pier along the new waterline. April 14, 1978. Courtesy of Port of Seattle

Things had calmed down at the University of Washington in the late 1970s. Here, two students heading for class pass the Henry Gallery. Horace C. Henry gave his art collection and $100,000 construction money to the university. The gallery was completed in 1927. Photograph by Lane Morgan; courtesy of Argus Magazine

The most influential Seattleite of the past thirty years has been a man who was in town so seldom that his voting address was a suite in the Olympic Hotel. Warren G. Magnuson's career in Congress ended after forty-four years with his loss to Slade Gorton in the 1980 election. While the election campaign was in progress, the Olympic itself was stripped of its furnishings and closed for renovation. It reopened in July, 1982. Courtesy of Argus Magazine

The Space Needle appears to be headed for the moon, or at least for an escape from the Seattle smog. The chimney is part of a laundry alongside Interstate 5. Courtesy of Tacoma News-Tribune *and* Associated Press

The Denny party in 1851 chose Alki Point for its settlement, anticipating that produce from farms along the Duwamish would attract shipping and would help the community grow. Instead, the valley became Seattle's industrial area. Arms of the freeway embrace the lower valley, the left arm reaching to West Seattle, the right curving around Boeing Field, skirting west of Beacon Hill, then looping behind the clustered towers of the Metropolis. Courtesy of Port of Seattle

BIBLIOGRAPHY

Bass, Sophie Frye. *Pig-Tail Days in Old Seattle*. Portland: Metropolitan Press, 1937.

Bagley, Clarence. *History of Seattle from the Earliest Settlement to the Present Time*. 3 vols. Chicago: S. J. Clarke Publishing Co., 1916.

Binns, Archie. *Northwest Gateway*. Portland: Binsford and Mort, 1941.

Burke, Padraic. *A History of the Port of Seattle*. Seattle: Port of Seattle, 1976.

Clark, Norman. *Washington: A Bicentennial History*. New York: W. W. Norton & Co., 1976.

Dorpat, Paul. *294 Glimpses*. Seattle: The Mayor's Task Force, 1981.

Faber, Jim. *An Irreverent Guide to Washington*. Garden City, N. Y.: Doubleday, 1974.

Hershman, Mark, Susan Heikkala, and Caroline Tobin. *Seattle's Waterfront: The Walker's Guide to the History of Elliott Bay*. Seattle: Waterfront Awareness, 1981.

Hines, Neal O. *Denny's Knoll: A History of the Metropolitan Tract of the University of Washington*. Seattle: University of Washington Press, 1980.

Morgan, Murray. *Skid Road: An Informal Portrait of Seattle*. New York: Viking Press, 1951.

Nesbit, Robert C. *"He Built Seattle": A Biography of Judge Thomas Burke*. Seattle: University of Washington Press, 1961.

Newell, Gordon. *Totem Tales of Old Seattle*. Seattle: Superior, 1956.

Quiett, Glenn Chesney. *They Built the West* (Chapter XV). New York: D. Appleton-Century Co., 1934.

Sale, Roger. *Seattle: Past to Present*. Seattle: University of Washington Press, 1976.

Speidel, Bill. *The Sons of the Profits*. Seattle: Nettle Creek Publishing Co., 1967.

Watt, Robert Frye. *Four Wagons West: The Story of Seattle*. Portland: Metropolitan Press, 1931.

Woodridge, Sally, and Roger Montgomery. *A Guide to Architecture in Washington State*. Seattle: University of Washington Press, 1980.

INDEX

Italicized numbers refer to page numbers of photos.